MATHS Problem-Solving Strategies

Author
Francis Teo

Executive Editor
Gan Yi Shen

Name: ____________________

Class: ____________________

MAHTS PROBLEM-SOLVING STRATEGIES BOOK 2

New Edition 2009

Published by Singapore Asian Publications (S) Pte Ltd

Distributed by

SINGAPORE (KELVIN YOO)
Singapore Asian Publications (S) Pte Ltd
219 Henderson Road #10-04,
Henderson Industrial Park Singapore 159556
Tel: (65) 6276 8280 Fax: (65) 6276 8292
E-mail: info@sapgrp.com
For order enquiries:
E-mail: kelvinyoo@sapgrp.com
Website: www.sapgrp.com

MALAYSIA (ANG WOOI KOK)
SAP Publications (M) Sdn Bhd
21, Jalan Industri USJ 1/3
Taman Perindustrian USJ 1,
47600 Subang Jaya, Selangor, Malaysia
Tel: (603) 8024 9962 Fax: (603) 8024 8231
E-mail: cs@sapgrp.com
For order enquiries:
E-mail: wkang@sapgrp.com

HONG KONG (DENNY KI)
SAP Publications (HK) Ltd
Office:
23 Nam Long Shan Road, Aberdeen, Hong Kong
Tel: (852) 2553 9188 Fax: (852) 2553 0099
Warehouse:
Flat 5, 11th Floor, Luen Cheong Can Centre,
6-8 Yip Wong Road, Tuen Mun, N.T., Hong Kong
Tel: (852) 2456 0233 Fax: (852) 2454 6148
E-mail: info@sapgrp.com
For order enquiries:
E-mail: dennyki@sapgrp.com

ISBN-13 978-981-255-768-1
ISBN-10 981-255-768-7

Printed in Singapore

GOOD BOOKS · OUR BUSINESS

The primary aim of **MATHS Problem-Solving Strategies Books 1-6** is to help pupils develop their mathematical thinking skills and expand their knowledge of mathematical concepts and formulae. Each book provides ample practice on various routine and practical mathematical problems.

The topics selected for each level are based on the latest syllabus. Examples of common word problems are given followed by the step-by-step working to show the process of problem solving. In **MATHS Problem-Solving Strategies Books 3-6**, notes are included. These notes highlight important and relevant mathematical concepts and formulae.

Challenging problems, which are indicated with asterisks, are also found in each topic. These challenge pupils to master their skill in higher-order thinking. Revision papers provide an overall assessment of the pupils' progress in learning these mathematical concepts.

Pupils will find this book useful in preparing for their examinations.

Francis Teo

Contents

Addition And Subtraction Within 1000

Example 1

Dan had some stamps. He gave 235 stamps to Eric, 149 stamps to Sam and had 162 stamps left. How many stamps did Dan have at first?

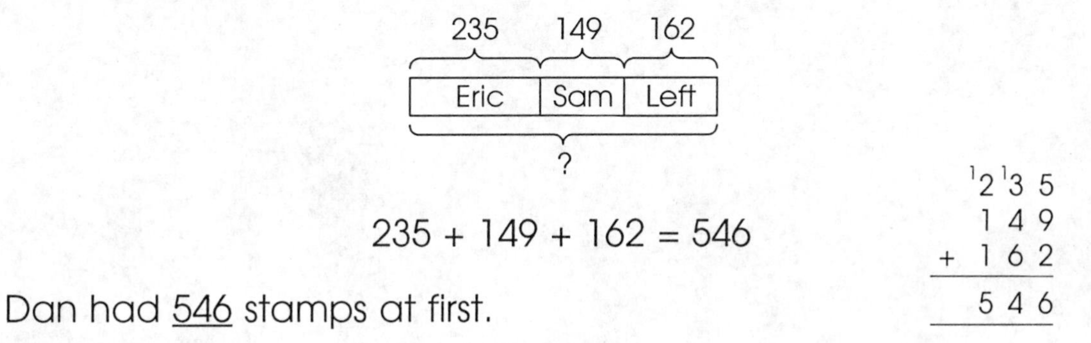

$$235 + 149 + 162 = 546$$

Dan had <u>546</u> stamps at first.

Example 2

There are 309 boys in a school. There are 246 more girls than boys in the school. How many pupils are there in the school?

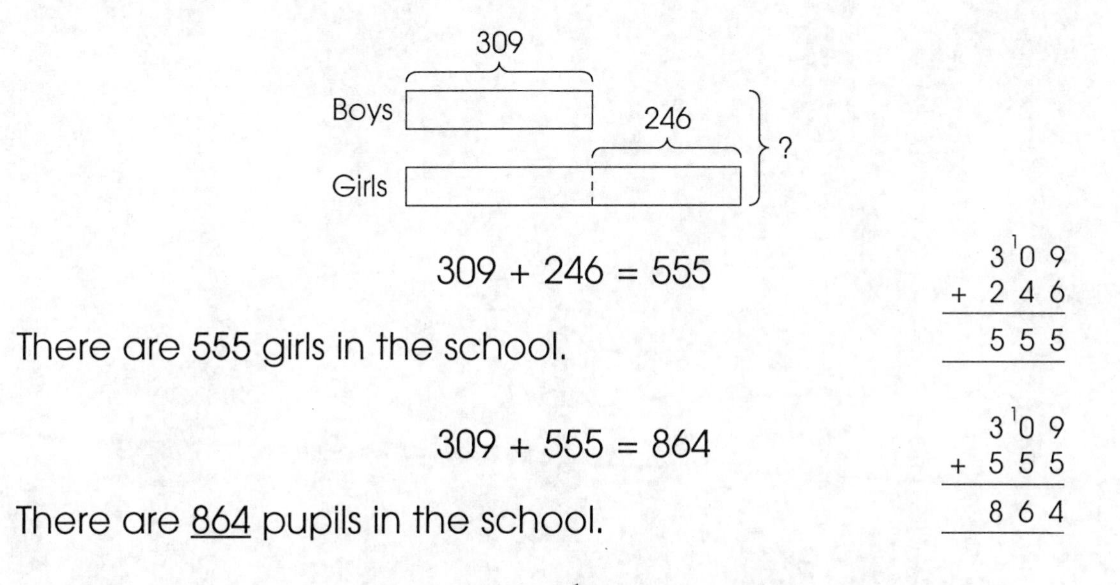

$$309 + 246 = 555$$

There are 555 girls in the school.

$$309 + 555 = 864$$

There are <u>864</u> pupils in the school.

PRACTICE

1. There are 397 boys and 504 girls in a school. How many pupils are there in the school?

2. Zoe had $900. She bought a television set and had $245 left. How much did the television set cost?

*3. Shirley had 405 blue beads and 398 red beads. She gave 142 beads to her friend. How many beads had she left?

4. Benny bought some paper clips. He gave 129 paper clips to Gerald and 294 paper clips to Tom. Benny then had 184 paper clips left. How many paper clips did Benny buy?

5. The difference between two numbers is 302. If the smaller number is 418, what is the larger number?

*6. A farmer has 740 chickens and ducks. If he has 257 ducks, how many more chickens than ducks are there?

7. A fishmonger sold 137 fish on Friday, 205 fish on Saturday and 492 fish on Sunday. How many fish did he sell altogether?

8. Peter bought 900 straws. After using some straws to weave a basket, he had 82 straws left. How many straws did he use to weave the basket?

9. Marian collected 407 stamps. She gave some stamps to Sophia and had 199 stamps left. How many stamps did Marian give to Sophia?

*10. The total savings of Paul, Adam and Samuel is $1000. Paul saved $247 and Adam saved $425. How much money did Samuel save?

*11.

✿ + 🍁 = 424

✿ + $\diamond$ = 455

$\diamond$ = 310

From the above information, find the value of 🍁.

12. Mr Lee sold 920 tarts in 3 days. He sold 359 tarts on the first day. How many tarts did he sell on the second and third day altogether?

Length

Example 1

Pete is 25 cm taller than Sally. Sally is 32 cm shorter than Molly. If Molly is 125 cm tall, find Pete's height.

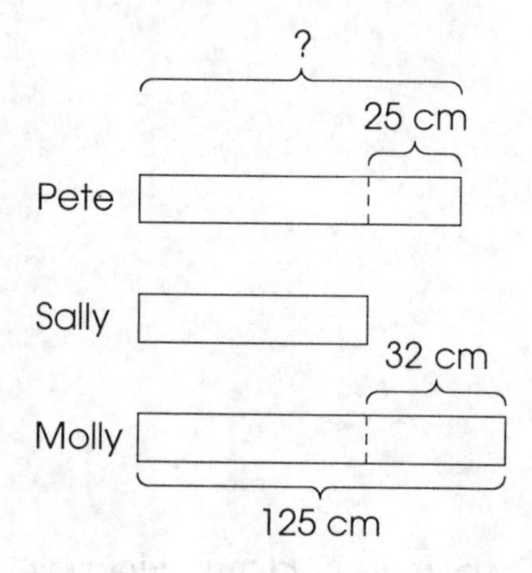

$$125 \text{ cm} - 32 \text{ cm} = 93 \text{ cm}$$

$$\begin{array}{r} \overset{0}{\cancel{1}}\overset{12}{\cancel{2}}5 \\ -\ \ 32 \\ \hline 93 \end{array}$$

Sally is 93 cm tall.

$$93 \text{ cm} + 25 \text{ cm} = 118 \text{ cm}$$

$$\begin{array}{r} 93 \\ +\ \ 25 \\ \hline 118 \end{array}$$

Pete's height is <u>118</u> cm.

Example 2

Ribbon A is 45 cm longer than Ribbon B. If Ribbon A is 240 cm long, find the total length of both ribbons.

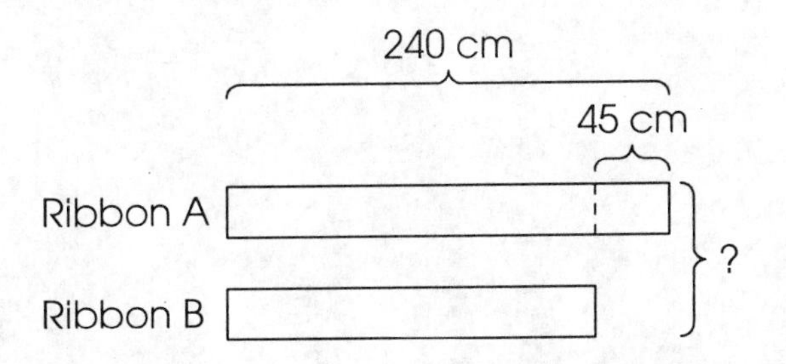

$$240\text{ cm} - 45\text{ cm} = 195\text{ cm}$$

$$\begin{array}{r} \overset{1}{\cancel{2}}\,\overset{13}{\cancel{4}}\,\overset{10}{\cancel{0}} \\ -\quad 4\;5 \\ \hline 1\;9\;5 \\ \hline \end{array}$$

Ribbon B is 195 cm long.

$$240\text{ cm} + 195\text{ cm} = 435\text{ cm}$$

$$\begin{array}{r} {}^{1}2\;4\;0 \\ +\,1\;9\;5 \\ \hline 4\;3\;5 \\ \hline \end{array}$$

The total length of both ribbons is <u>435</u> cm.

PRACTICE

1. Ronald is 94 cm tall. If Ronald is 16 cm shorter than James, find James' height.

*2. A yellow ribbon is 25 cm longer than a red ribbon. If the yellow ribbon is 77 cm long, find the total length of the two ribbons.

3. Kelvin ran a distance of 358 m and walked a distance of 499 m. Find the total distance he travelled.

*4. Barry is 13 cm taller than Jeff. Pete is 29 cm shorter than Barry. If Jeff is 102 cm tall, find Pete's height.

5. A hill is 425 m high. David climbs up the hill to a height of 197 m. How much further must David climb to reach the top of the hill?

*6. The total length of Pole A and Pole B is 640 cm. If Pole A is 294 cm long, how much longer is Pole B than Pole A?

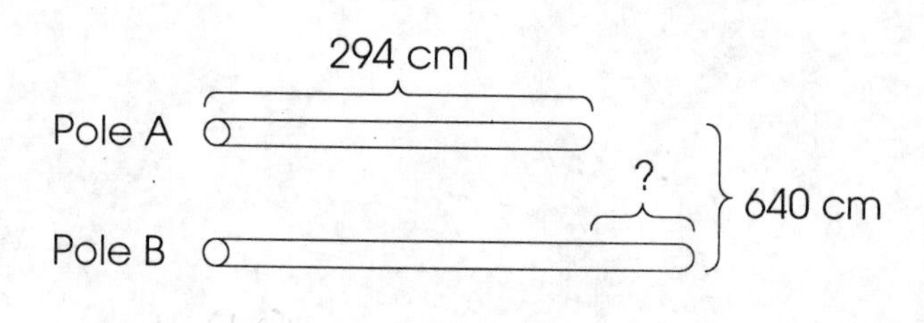

7. A wire was 243 cm long. It was cut into 3 pieces. The first piece was 75 cm long and the second piece was 109 cm long. Find the length of the third piece.

8.

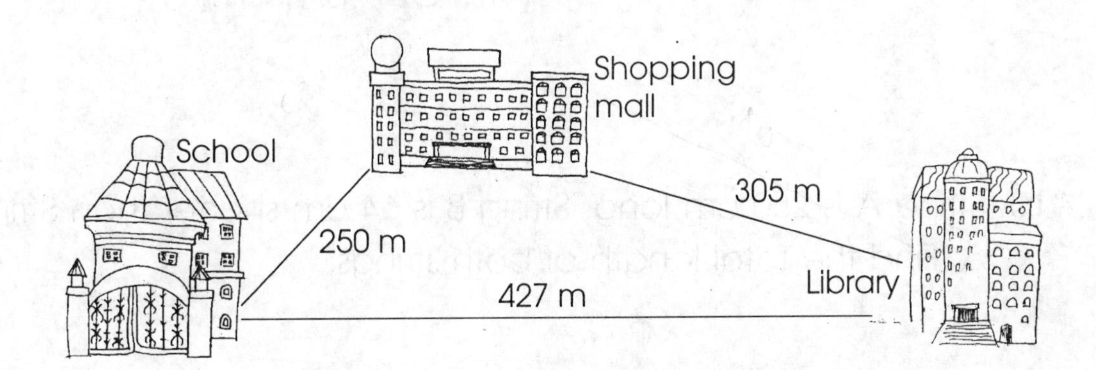

Cindy walked from school to the shopping mall, and then to the library. Jason walked from school directly to the library. How much farther did Cindy walk than Jason?

*9. A wooden plank was painted with 3 different colours. 97 cm of it was painted red, part of it was painted yellow and 49 cm of it was painted blue. If the wooden plank was 200 cm long, find the length of the part that was painted yellow.

*10. String A is 250 cm long. String B is 64 cm shorter than String A. Find the total length of both strings.

Use the information given in this picture to answer questions 11 and 12.

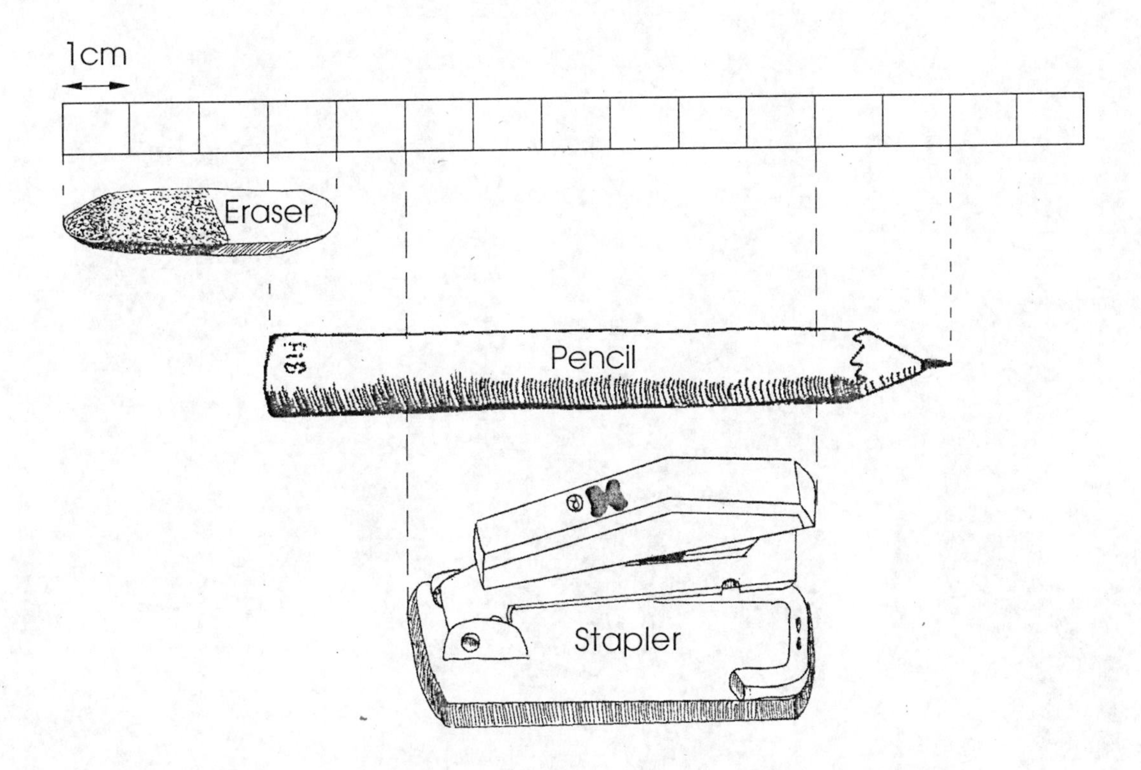

11. Find the total length of the eraser and the stapler.

12. How much longer is the pencil than the stapler?

Mass

Example 1

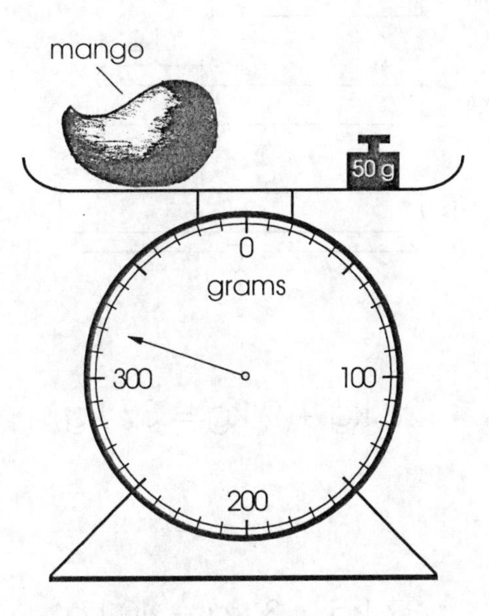

What is the mass of the mango?

320 g	
Mango	50 g

$$320 \text{ g} - 50 \text{ g} = 270 \text{ g}$$

```
  2 12
  3 2 0
-   5 0
-------
  2 7 0
```

The mass of the mango is <u>270</u> g.

Example 2

Phil's mass is 28 kg. Ken is heavier than Phil by 9 kg. Chris is 3 kg heavier than Ken. What is Chris' weight?

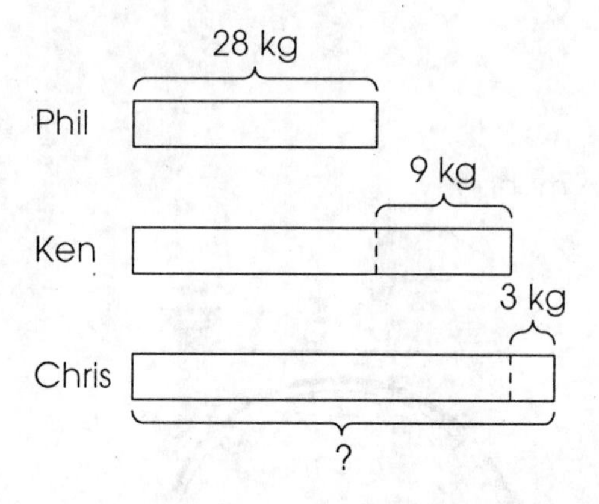

$$28\text{ kg} + 9\text{ kg} = 37\text{ kg}$$

$$\begin{array}{r} {}^{1}2\,8 \\ +\quad 9 \\ \hline 3\,7 \\ \hline \end{array}$$

Ken is 37 kg.

$$37\text{ kg} + 3\text{ kg} = 40\text{ kg}$$

$$\begin{array}{r} {}^{1}3\,7 \\ +\quad 3 \\ \hline 4\,0 \\ \hline \end{array}$$

Chris' weight is <u>40</u> kg.

PRACTICE

1. A bottle of oil has a mass of 925 g. When the bottle is empty, it has a mass of 185 g. Find the mass of the oil.

2. The total mass of a bicycle and a tricycle is 127 kg. If the bicycle has a mass of 75 kg, what is the mass of the tricycle?

3.

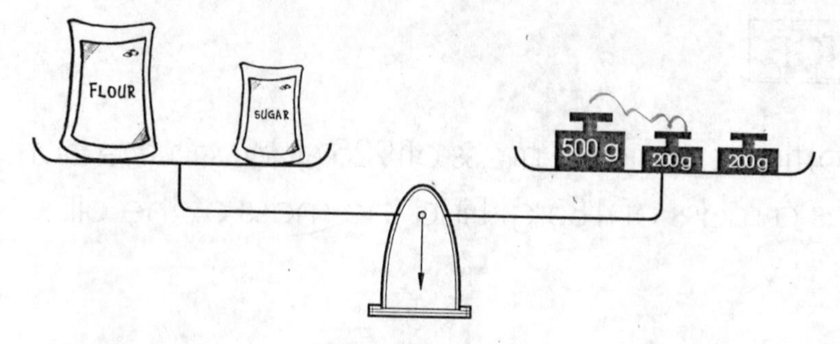

In the picture above, the mass of the packet of flour is 725 g. Find the mass of the packet of sugar.

*4. The total mass of Michelle and Tom is 82 kg. If Michelle's mass is 39 kg, how much heavier is Tom than Michelle?

5. The mass of the bunch of bananas is 520 g. Find the mass of the mango.

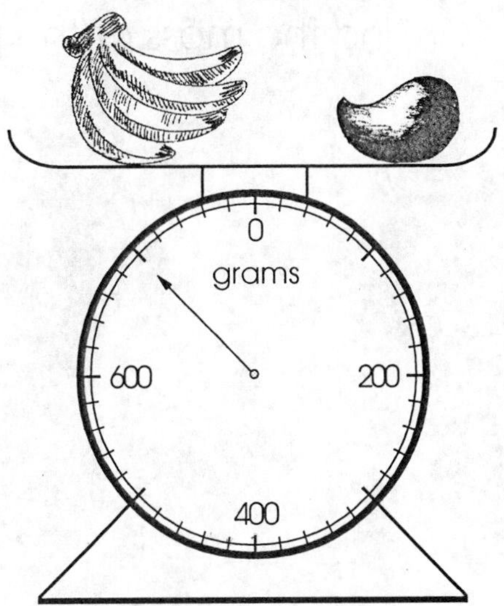

6. What is the mass of the brick?

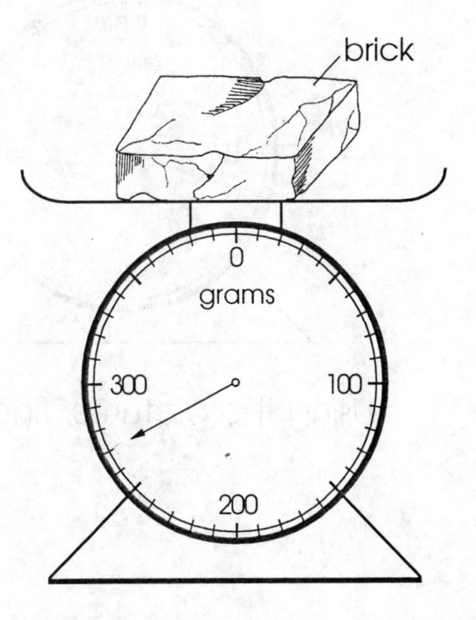

*7. The total mass of a packet of rice and a packet of flour is 24 kg. The packet of rice is 8 kg heavier than the packet of flour. Find the mass of the packet of rice.

*8.

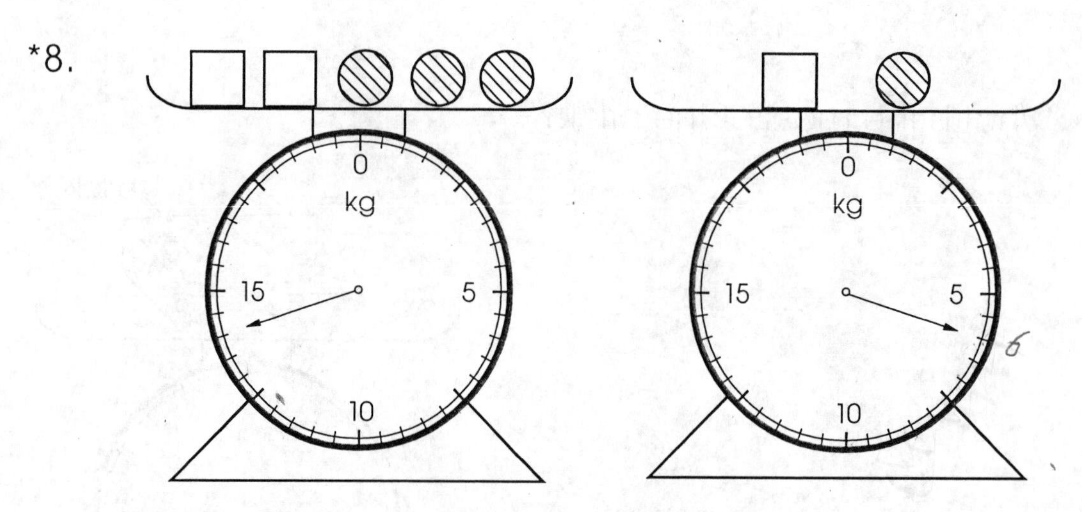

Using the pictures, find the mass of ◍.

9. Mrs Lee bought 320 g of grapes. She bought 180 g more strawberries than grapes. Find the total mass of the grapes and strawberries that Mrs Lee bought.

10. Kelly is 12 kg lighter than Barry. Susan is 29 kg heavier than Kelly. If Susan's mass is 50 kg, find Barry's mass.

*11. The total mass of Sally and Peter is 59 kg. If Sally's mass is 24 kg, how much heavier is Peter than Sally?

*12. When a glass is half filled with water, it has a mass of 510 g. When the glass is completely filled with water, its mass is 750 g. Find the mass of the glass when it is empty.

Multiplication And Division (Tables Of 2 And 3)

Example 1

27 sweets are shared equally among 3 girls. How many sweets does each girl receive?

27

Girl	Girl	Girl

?

$$27 \div 3 = 9$$

Each girl receives 9 sweets.

Example 2

Mrs Kent bought 3 packets of oranges. There were 10 oranges in each packet. She gave away 14 oranges. How many oranges had she left?

10	10	10
Oranges	Oranges	Oranges

$$3 \times 10 = 30$$

Mrs Kent bought 30 oranges.

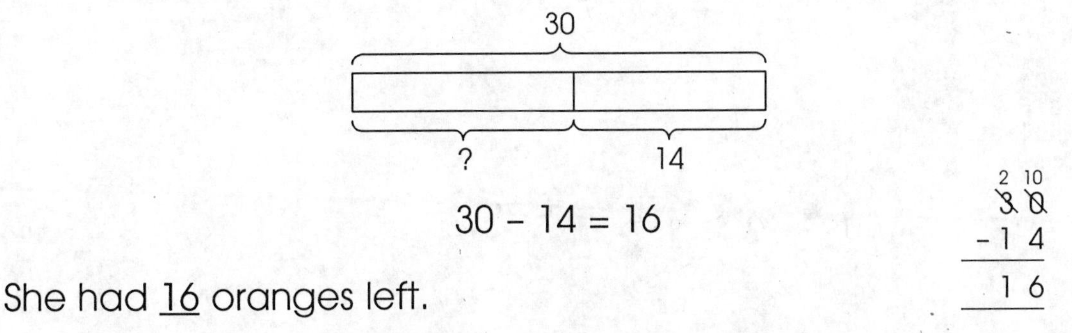

$$30 - 14 = 16$$

$$\begin{array}{r} \overset{2}{\not{3}}\,\overset{10}{\not{0}} \\ -\ 1\ 4 \\ \hline 1\ 6 \end{array}$$

She had 16 oranges left.

PRACTICE

1. During a football match, 18 boys are grouped into 2 teams. How many boys are there in each team?

2. 21 cookies are shared equally among 3 girls. How many cookies does each girl receive?

3. Maureen shares 18 stickers with two of her friends. How many stickers does Maureen receive?

4. Mrs Wilson bought 3 packets of apples. There were 9 apples in each packet. How many apples did Mrs Wilson buy altogether?

*5. David had 14 marbles. He bought 16 more marbles. He then put all his marbles equally into 3 boxes. How many marbles were there in each box?

*6. Mary bought 2 boxes of chicken pies. Each box contained 9 chicken pies. She ate 3 chicken pies. How many chicken pies were left?

*7. A carpenter needs 3 screws to fix a stool. He has 35 screws. After fixing 8 stools, how many screws has he left?

8. Larry eats 2 eggs a day. How many eggs does he eat in one week?

9. Mervyn has some tricycles. Each tricycle has 3 wheels. Mervyn counts the wheels of his tricycles and finds that there are 12 wheels altogether. How many tricycles does Mervyn have?

*10. There are 12 girls and 6 boys in a classroom. The pupils are arranged into groups of 3. How many groups are there?

*11. There were 3 adults and 7 children at a birthday party. Each person ate 2 pieces of cake. After all the guests had eaten, 29 pieces of cake were left. How many pieces of cake were there at first?

12. There are 3 chairs to every table at a coffee shop. If there are 21 chairs, how many tables are there?

Money

Example 1

Mr Stokes had 3 ten-dollar notes and 2 five-dollar notes. He bought a wallet for $21. How much money had he left?

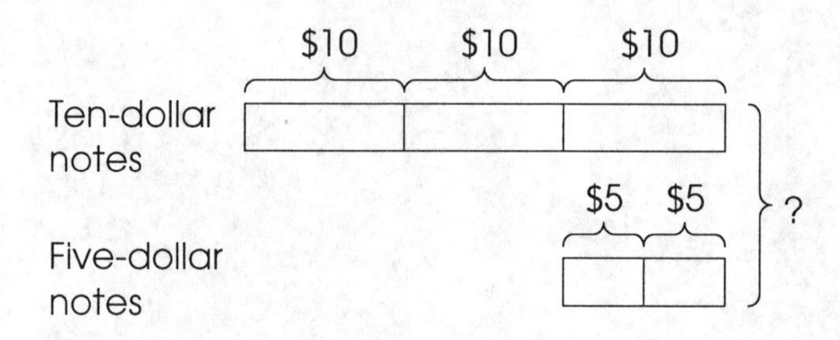

3 ten-dollar notes = 3 × $10
= $30

2 five-dollar notes = 2 × $5
= $10

$30 + $10 = $40

```
  $30
+ $10
-----
  $40
```

Mr Stokes had $40.

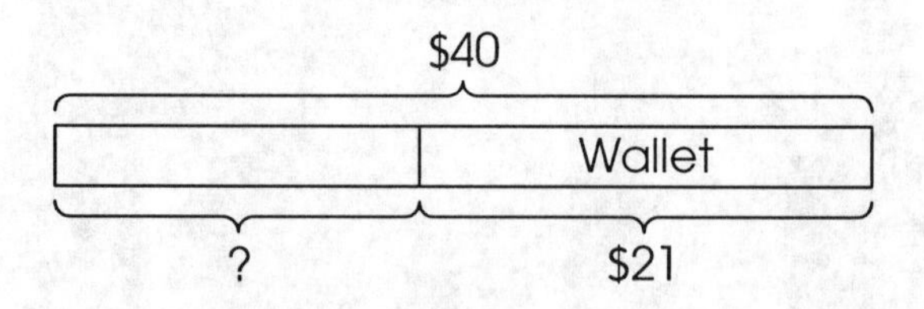

$40 – $21 = $19

```
   3 10
  $4 0
- $2 1
------
  $1 9
```

He had $<u>19</u> left.

Example 2

Kelly had $29.70. She bought a storybook for $13. How much money had she left?

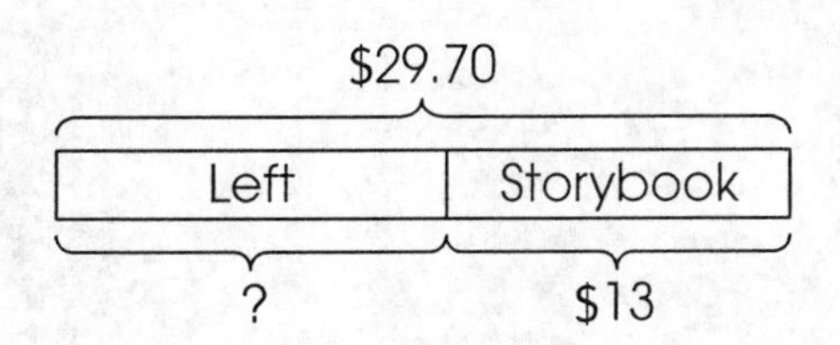

$$\$29.70 - \$13 = \$16.70$$

```
  $29.70
- $13.00
  $16.70
```

She had $\underline{16.70}$ left.

PRACTICE

1. Mandy had $7.30. She spent some money on food and had $0.30 left. How much money did she spend on food?

*2. Charles had $40. He bought a storybook for $16 and a pen. If the storybook cost $12 more than the pen, how much money had Charles left?

3. Alex saved 90¢ more than Linda. If Linda saved \$8.25, how much money did Alex save?

4. Mr Winston bought a cake for \$17.50. He gave the cashier two ten-dollar notes. How much change did he receive?

*5. A hamburger costs $1. A chicken burger costs 60¢ more than the hamburger. Find the total cost of both items.

*6. Dennis had $9 and Paul had $5.90. Dennis spent $6 while Paul spent 50¢. How much more money had Paul left than Dennis?

*7. Elsie had $10 and Xavier had $7.70. Each of them bought a similar can of soft drink. Elsie then had $9.50 left. How much money had Xavier left?

8. Mia has 2 fifty-cent coins, 3 twenty-cent coins and 3 five-cent coins. How much money does she have?

9. A papaya costs $2.70. A watermelon costs $0.45 more than the papaya. How much does the watermelon cost?

*10. Monica has 5 coins. Their total value is 55¢. How many ten-cent coins does Monica have?

*11. Durians were sold at 2 for $3. Mrs Thomson bought 16 durians. How much did she pay for the durians?

*12. $27 is shared equally among Susan, Jacky and Tom. How much money do Jacky and Tom receive altogether?

General Revision 1

1. There are 495 boys and 379 girls in a school. 147 pupils wear spectacles. How many pupils do not wear spectacles?

2. Martin had $750. He bought a camera for $379 and a pair of shoes for $95. How much money had Martin left?

*3. A farmer had 974 eggs. He broke 29 eggs, sold some of them and had 162 eggs left. How many eggs did he sell?

4. Allen collected 142 seashells. Paul collected 55 fewer seashells than Allen. How many seashells did both boys collect altogether?

5. The sum of the length and breadth of a rectangular desk is 92 cm. If its length is 57 cm, find its breadth.

6. Find the total length of the pen and the pair of scissors

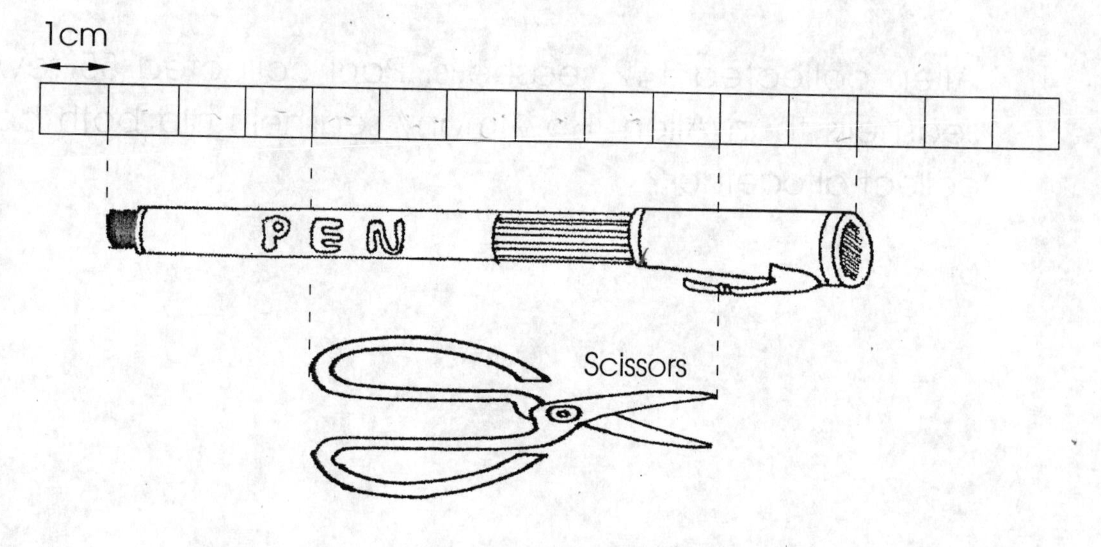

*7. The mass of a car is 870 kg. When Mr and Mrs Lee are in the car, the total mass is 995 kg. If Mr Lee has a mass of 72 kg, find Mrs Lee's mass.

8. The mass of 3 similar bags of rice is 21 kg. Find the mass of 2 bags of rice.

*9. Daniel bought 3 boxes of handkerchiefs. There were 3 handkerchiefs in each box. If each handkerchief cost $2, how much did Daniel spend on the handkerchiefs?

10. 6 teams of badminton players participated at a competition. There were 2 badminton players in each team. How many badminton players participated at the competition?

11. Laura had $12. She spent 30¢ on sweets and 70¢ on drinks. How much money had she left?

12. Keith wants to buy a storybook that costs $7.45. He has $5. How much more money does he need?

General Revision 2

1. Mark had 145 marbles. He gave 39 marbles to George and 47 marbles to Nick. How many marbles had Mark left?

*2. There are 195 more boys than girls in a school. If there are 452 boys in the school, how many pupils are there in the school?

*3. The total cost of a T-shirt and a jacket is $23. If the jacket costs $5 more than the T-shirt, find the cost of the T-shirt.

4. A durian seller sold 102 durians on Friday, 295 durians on Saturday and 340 durians on Sunday. How many durians did he sell in the 3 days?

5. How many times longer is the pencil than the eraser?

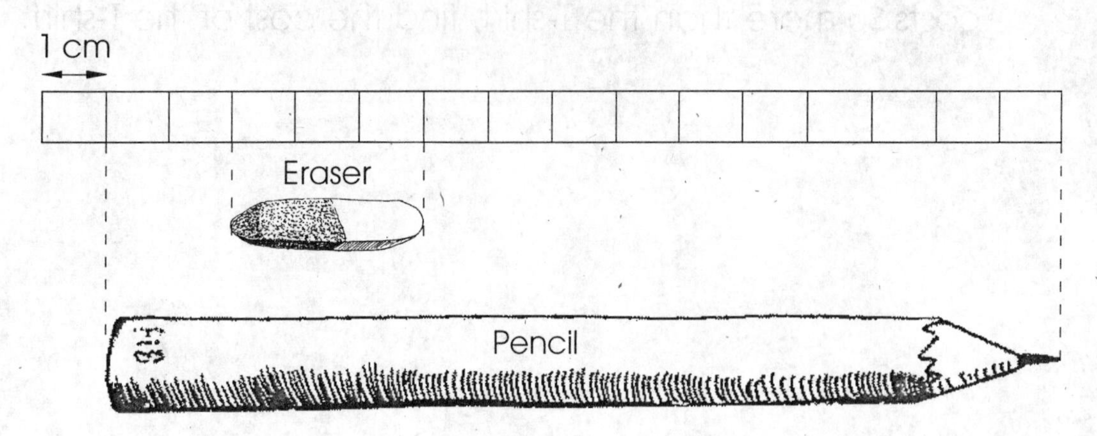

6. Ken is 13 cm taller than Roy. Mary is 24 cm shorter than Roy. How much taller is Ken than Mary?

7.

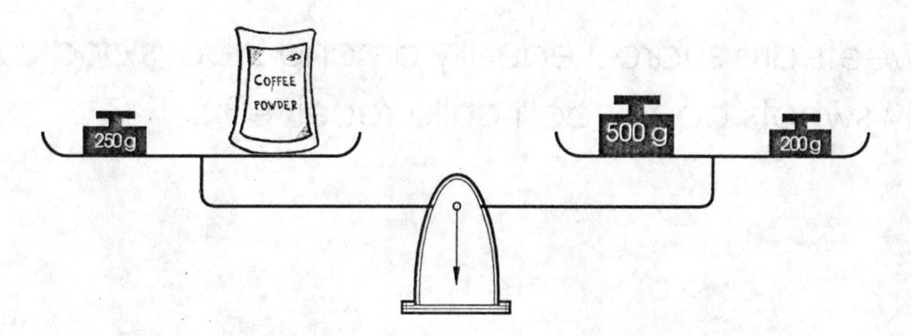

Find the mass of the packet of coffee powder in the above picture.

*8. The total mass of Jerald, William and Irene is 74 kg. Jerald's mass is 27 kg. William is 4 kg heavier than Jerald. What is Irene's mass?

9. 24 sweets are shared equally among 2 boys and a girl. How many sweets does each child receive?

10. At a birthday party, each guest ate 2 pieces of cake. Altogether, 18 pieces of cake were eaten. How many guests were there at the party?

*11. Lucy had $3.90. Julie had $4 more than Lucy. Julie bought a packet of tissue paper for 35¢. How much money had she left?

12. A slice of watermelon costs $0.60. A stick of jackfruits costs $0.70. Find the total cost of the slice of watermelon and the stick of jackfruits.

Multiplication And Division (Tables Of 4, 5 And 10)

Example 1

Mrs Winter bought 5 cakes. She cut each cake into 8 equal pieces. If she ate 3 pieces of cake, how many pieces of cake had she left?

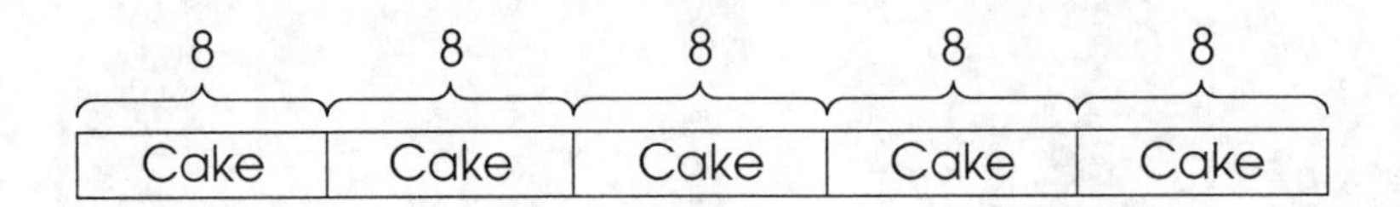

$$5 \times 8 = 40$$

There were 40 pieces of cake.

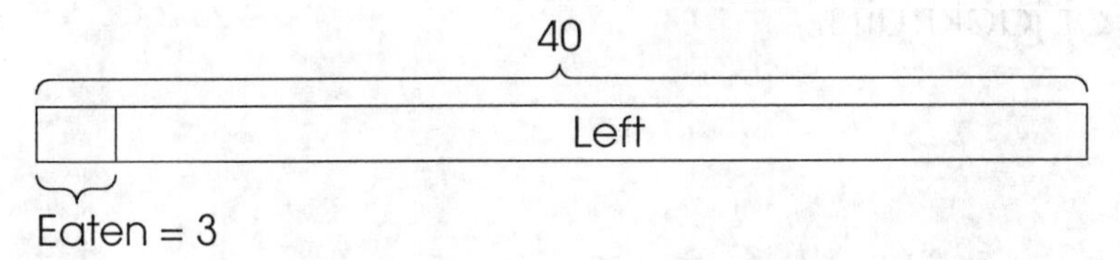

$$40 - 3 = 37$$

$$\begin{array}{r} \overset{3}{\cancel{4}}\,\overset{10}{\cancel{0}} \\ -\quad 3 \\ \hline 3\,7 \\ \hline \end{array}$$

She had <u>37</u> pieces of cake left.

Example 2

The cost of 9 similar T-shirts is \$45. Find the cost of 4 such T-shirts.

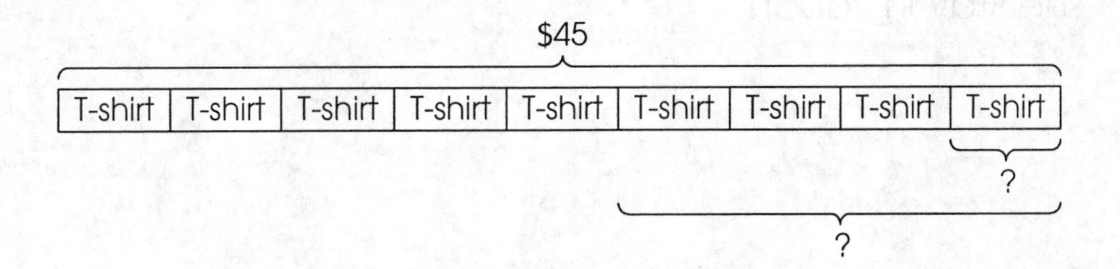

$$\$45 \div 9 = \$5$$

1 shirt costs \$5.

$$4 \times \$5 = \$20$$

The cost of 4 such T-shirts is \$<u>20</u>.

PRACTICE

1. Mrs Trent stayed in Japan for 4 weeks. How many days did she stay in Japan?

*2. Larry bought 5 bundles of pencils. There were 8 pencils in each bundle. If he gave 12 pencils to his friends, how many pencils had he left?

3. There are 9 benches at a park. Each bench can seat 5 people. How many people can be seated at the park at one time?

45

45 people can be seated

*4. 4 boys and 3 girls shared the cost of a present equally. If the present cost $35, how much did each of them pay?

$5

5. Anna bought 45 cm of ribbon. She cut it into equal pieces. Each piece was 5 cm long. How many pieces did Anna have?

*6. Martin has $59. He buys 6 bottles of chocolate milk. If each bottle costs $4, how much money has he left?

*7. Julie bought some pens at $7 each. She gave the cashier a hundred-dollar note and received a change of $72. How many pens did she buy?

8. Nine good friends donated $10 each to an orphanage. How much money did they donate to the orphanage altogether?

9. The cost of 4 similar wallets is $40. Find the cost of 3 such wallets.

*10. Kenny has 9 five-cent coins and 8 ten-cent coins. Find the total value of Kenny's coins.

11. Mary baked 4 cakes. She cut each cake into 9 pieces. How many pieces of cake did she have?

*12. Mrs Blake bought 4 large durians at $6 each and 5 small durians at $4 each. She gave the fruit seller a fifty-dollar note. How much change did she receive?

Fractions

Example 1

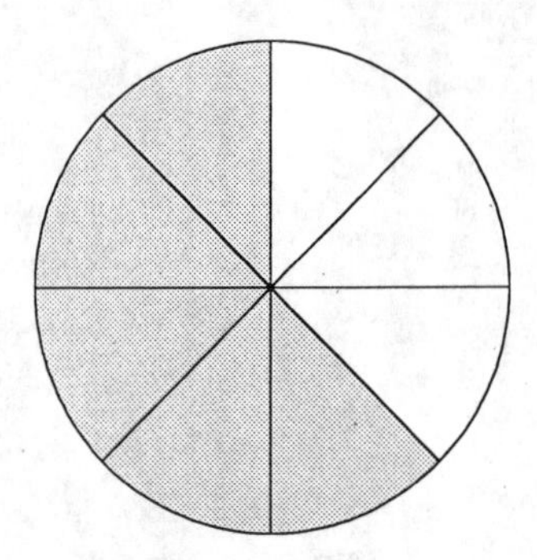

5 parts out of 8 equal parts of this circle are shaded.

Therefore, $\frac{5}{8}$ of the circle is shaded.

Example 2

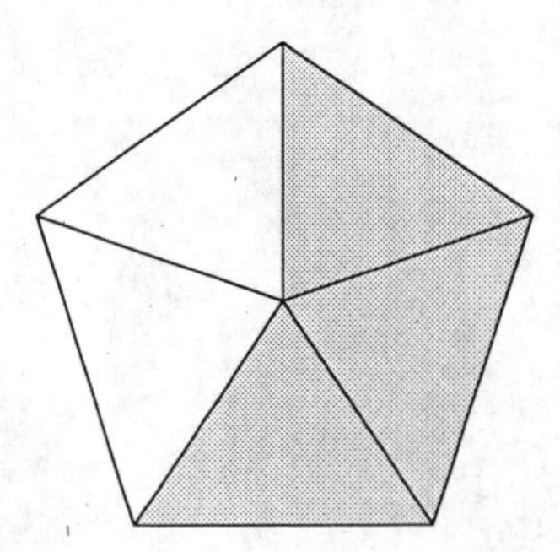

2 parts out of 5 equal parts of this figure are not shaded.

Therefore, $\frac{2}{5}$ of the figure is not shaded.

PRACTICE

1.

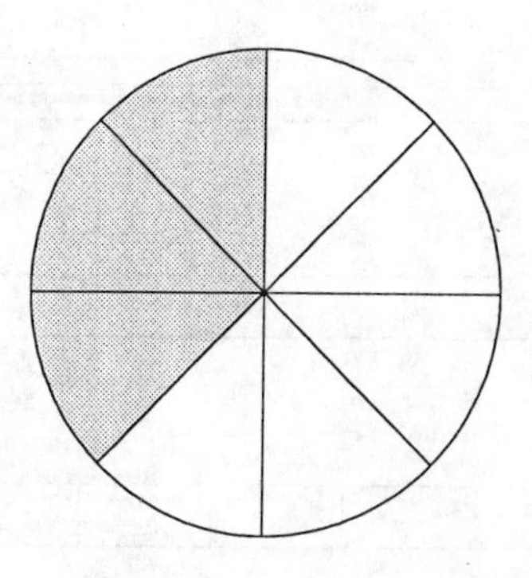

__________ of the circle is shaded.

__________ out of __________ equal parts are shaded.

2.

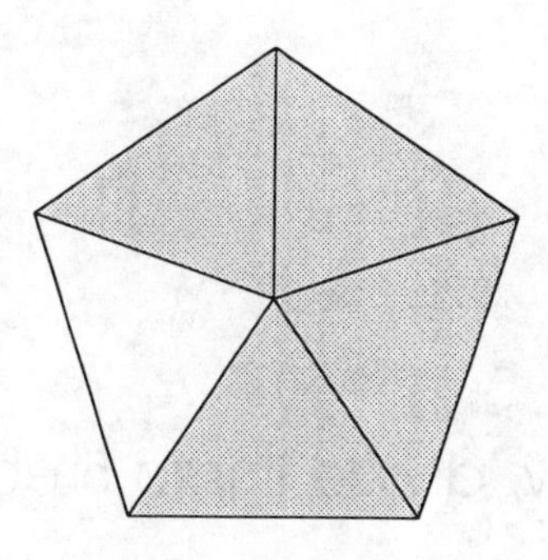

__________ of the figure is shaded.

__________ out of __________ equal parts are shaded.

For each of the following bars, shade the correct number of parts to show the given fraction.

3. $\frac{3}{4}$

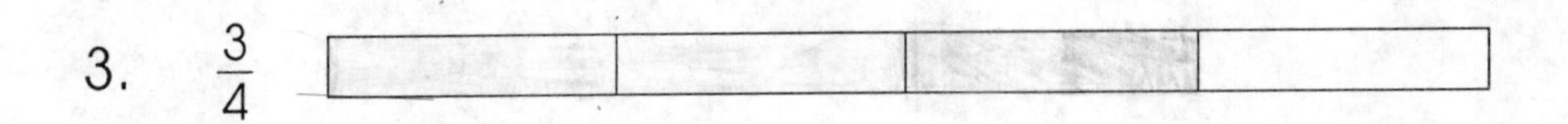

4. $\frac{2}{5}$

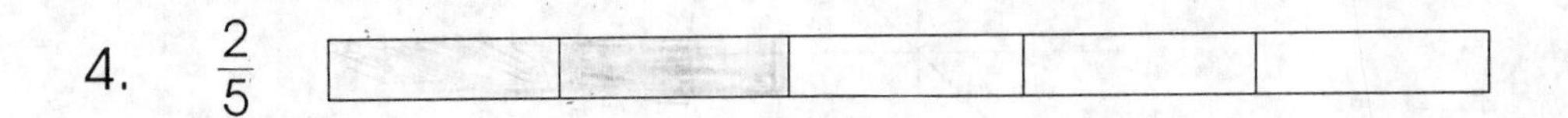

5. $\frac{5}{9}$

6. For the bar below, divide it into 4 equal parts and shade one part.

What fraction of the bar is shaded?

7. For the bar below, divide it into 5 equal parts and shade 3 parts.

What fraction of the bar is shaded?

8. Shade $\frac{3}{7}$ of this bar.

For questions 9 to 11, shade the correct fraction for each bar and circle the largest fraction.

9. $\frac{4}{5}$

$\frac{1}{5}$

$\frac{3}{5}$

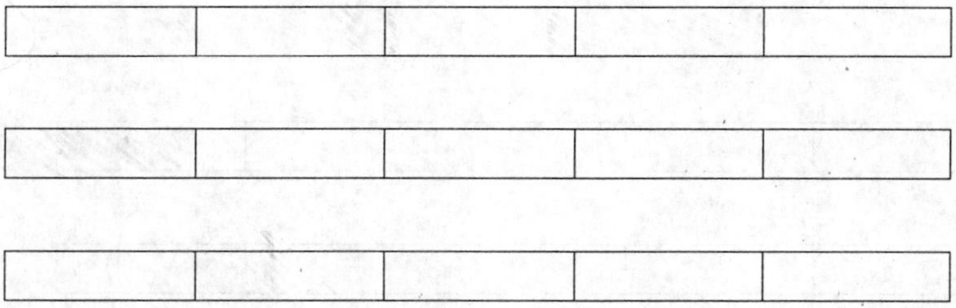

10. $\frac{1}{3}$

$\frac{1}{2}$

$\frac{1}{5}$

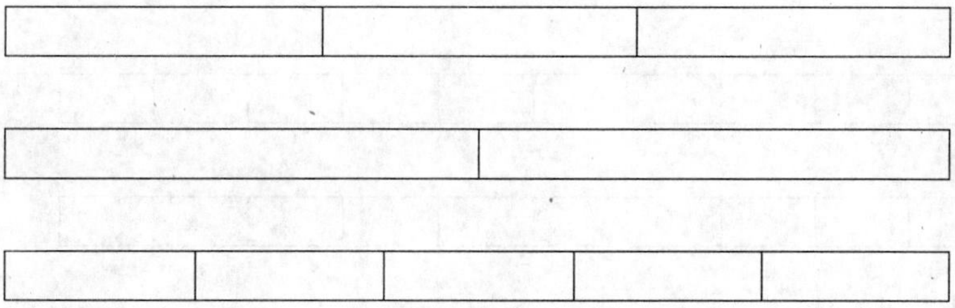

11. $\frac{2}{9}$

$\frac{7}{9}$

$\frac{3}{9}$

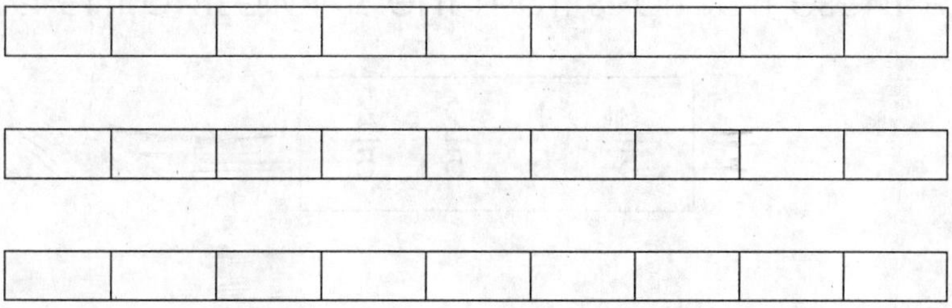

For questions 12 to 14, shade the correct fraction for each bar and circle the smallest fraction.

12. $\frac{1}{6}$

$\frac{1}{10}$

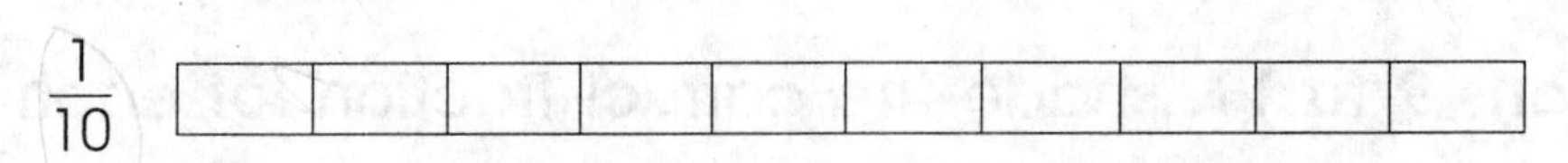

$\frac{1}{4}$

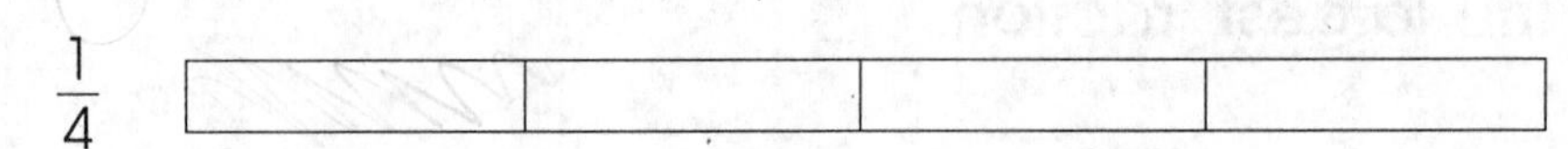

13. $\frac{3}{5}$

$\frac{1}{5}$

$\frac{4}{5}$

14. $\frac{5}{10}$

$\frac{3}{10}$

$\frac{7}{10}$

15. Arrange these fractions from the smallest to the biggest.

$\frac{3}{5}$ $\frac{1}{5}$ $\frac{2}{5}$ $\frac{4}{5}$

16. How many quarters are there in a whole?

17. Which of the following fractions is the smallest?

$\frac{1}{7}$	$\frac{2}{7}$	$\frac{1}{9}$	$\frac{1}{5}$

18. Hilda bought a cake. After cutting it into 8 equal pieces, she ate 3 pieces. What fraction of the cake had she eaten?

*19. $\frac{4}{9}$ of a circle is shaded. What fraction of the circle is not shaded?

*20. There are 12 pupils in a classroom. 5 of them are boys. What fraction of the pupils are girls?

Time

Example 1

This clock is half an hour slow. What is the actual time?

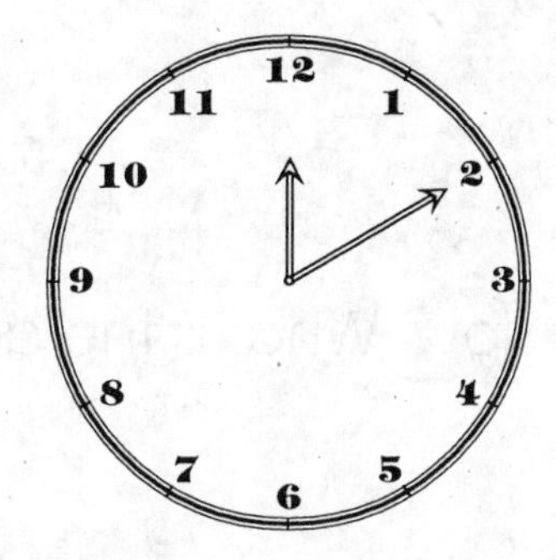

12.10 + 30 min = 12.40

```
  12.10
+    30
-------
  12.40
```

The actual time is 12.40.

Example 2

A musical show began at 7.30 p.m. and ended at 9.00 p.m. How long did the musical show last?

30 min   1 h

7.30 p.m.   8.00 p.m.   9.00 p.m.

1 h + 30 min = 1 h 30 min

```
  1 h 00 min
+     30 min
------------
  1 h 30 min
```

The musical show lasted for 1 h and 30 min.

PRACTICE

1. This clock is 1 h slow. What is the actual time?

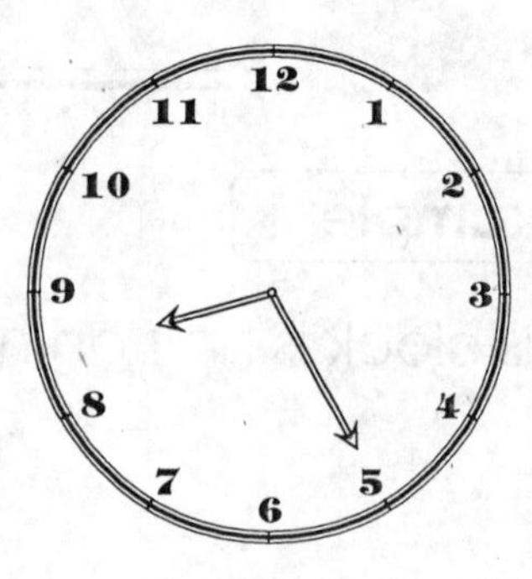

2. This clock is 30 min slow. What is the actual time?

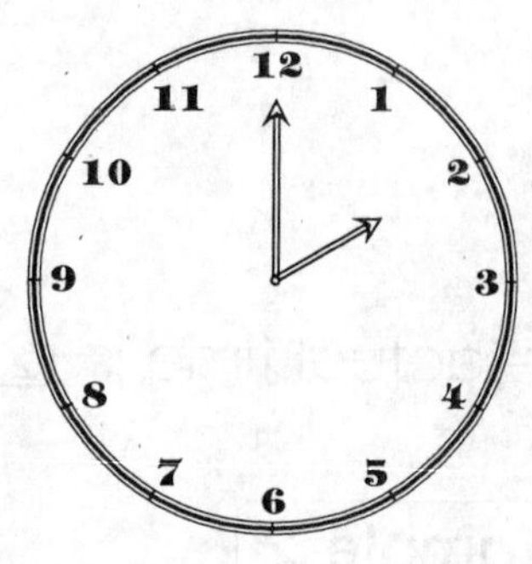

3. This clock is 10 min fast. What is the actual time?

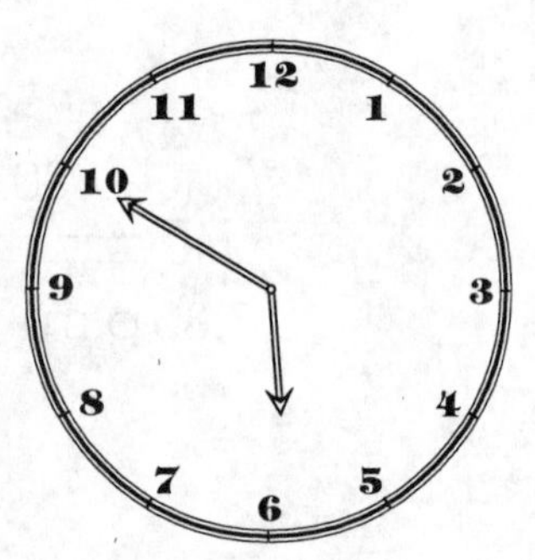

4. How many minutes are there between 10.45 and 11.30?

5. Jason cycled for 1 h. He finished cycling at 7.30 a.m. At what time did he begin cycling?

6. A movie began at 8.20 p.m. It lasted for 2 h. At what time did the movie end?

*7. An English test lasted for 1 h 20 minutes. It ended at 11.00 a.m. At what time did the English test begin?

8. A coach left Town A at 9 a.m. and reached Town B at 2 p.m. How many hours did the coach travel?

*9. Melvin began jogging at 6.20 a.m. He jogged for 50 min. At what time did he complete his jogging?

10. Lucy's grandmother took a half-hour afternoon nap. She slept at 3.50 p.m. At what time did she wake up?

11. Derrick's watch is 20 min slow. If the actual time is 11.30 p.m., what is the time shown on Derrick's watch?

*12. Alfred began doing his homework at 8:30 p.m. He completed his homework at 10:15 p.m. How many hours and minutes did he take to complete his homework?

Volume

Example 1

Mavis poured 6 bottles of water into an empty pail. Each bottle contained 4 ℓ of water. She then used 7 ℓ of water from the pail to water the plants. How many litres of water were left in the pail?

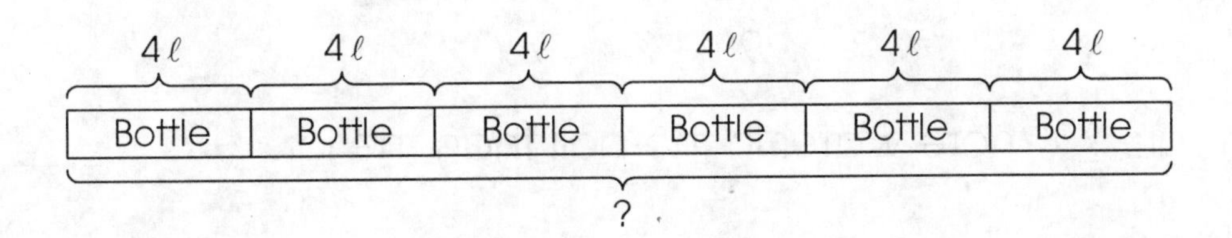

$$6 \times 4\ \ell = 24\ \ell$$

Mavis poured 24 ℓ of water into the pail.

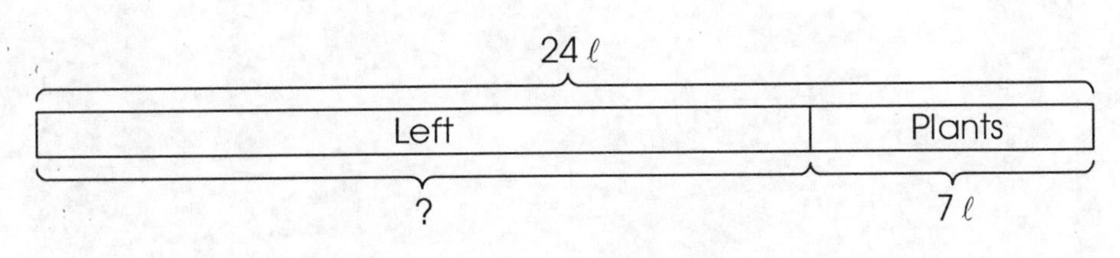

$$24\ \ell - 7\ \ell = 17\ \ell$$

$$\begin{array}{r} {}^{1}\not{2}\,{}^{14}\not{4} \\ -\quad 7 \\ \hline 1\,7 \\ \hline \end{array}$$

<u>17</u> ℓ of water were left in the pail.

Example 2

A jar contains 2 ℓ of water. A pail contains 9 ℓ of water. How many more litres of water are there in the pail than the jar?

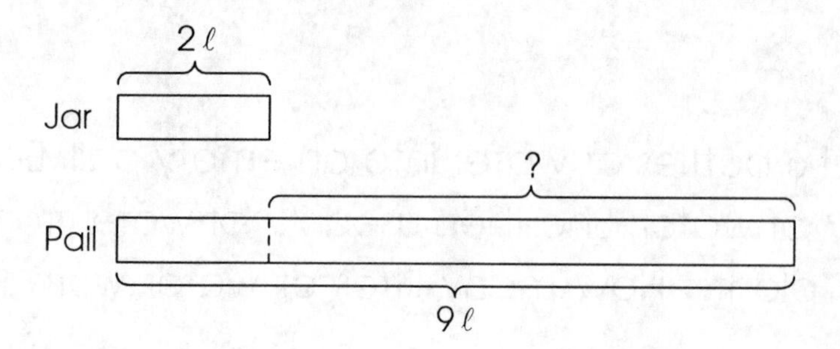

$$9\ \ell - 2\ \ell = 7\ \ell$$

$$\begin{array}{r} 9 \\ -\ 2 \\ \hline 7 \end{array}$$

There are <u>7</u> ℓ more water in the pail than the jar.

PRACTICE

Study the pictures carefully. Use the information to answer questions 1 to 4.

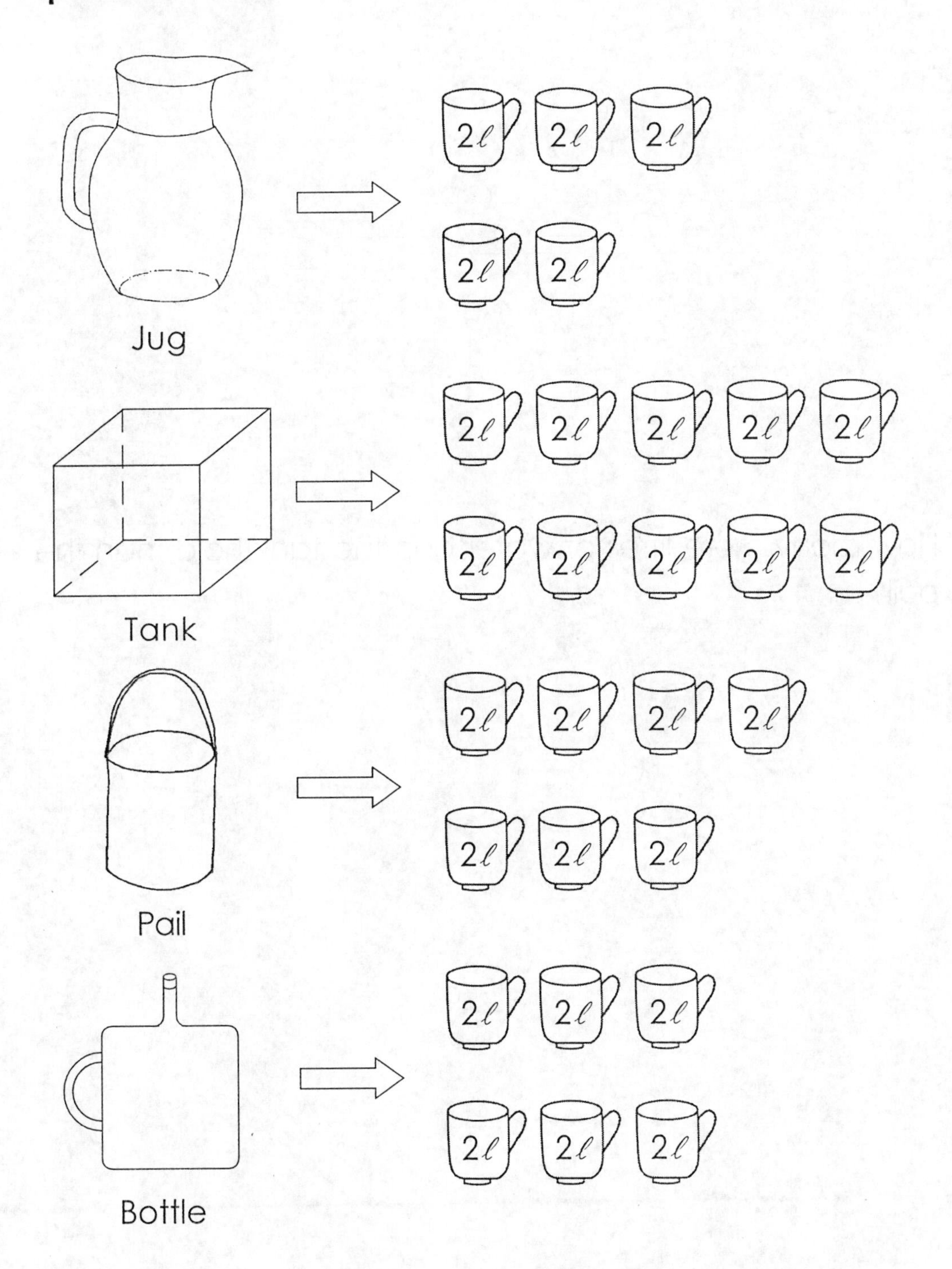

1. How many litres of water can the jug hold?

2. How many more litres of water can the tank hold than the pail?

3. The tank can hold ______________ times as much water as the jug.

4. Find the total capacity of the tank, the pail and the bottle.

5. David bought 9 tins of paint. Each tin contained 4 ℓ of paint. He used 24 ℓ of paint. How many litres of paint had he left?

*6. Tank A contains 32 ℓ more water than Tank B. If Tank A contains 65 ℓ of water, find the total amount of water in both tanks.

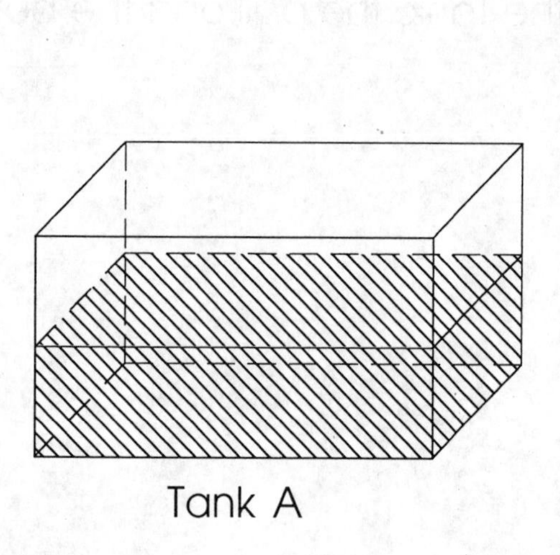
Tank A

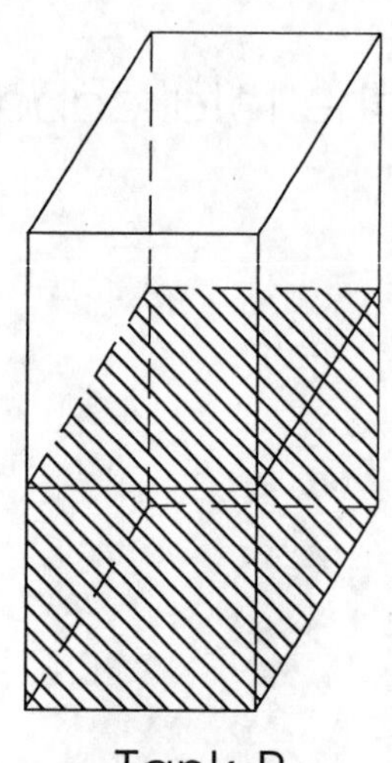
Tank B

7. Mary mixed 12 ℓ of orange juice with 9 ℓ of lemon juice. She then accidentally spilled 5 ℓ of the mixed fruit juice. How many litres of mixed fruit juice had she left?

*8. Mrs Andrews bought 5 large tins and 9 small tins of oil. Each large tin contains 10 ℓ of oil and each small tin contains 5 ℓ of oil. How many litres of oil did Mrs Andrews buy altogether?

*9. Serene had 40 ℓ of chocolate drink. She poured the chocolate drink equally into 7 bottles and had 5 ℓ left over. How many litres of chocolate drink were there in each bottle?

*10. Mr Woods bought 4 similar tins of petrol. He used up 20 ℓ of petrol and had 16 ℓ of it left. How many litres of petrol were there in each tin?

*11. A pail and a basin contain 24 ℓ of water altogether. If the pail contains 4 ℓ more water than the basin, how many litres of water are there in the basin?

12. Five similar pails can hold 20 ℓ of water altogether. How many litres of water can 2 such pails hold?

Graphs

Example 1

The graph shows the weight of cherries sold by a fruiterer. Study the graph carefully and answer the questions.

Monday	
Tuesday	
Wednesday	
Thursday	
Friday	
Saturday	
Each	stands for 3 kg of cherries.

How many kg of cherries were sold on Friday and Saturday?

$$4 \times 3 \text{ kg} = 12 \text{ kg}$$

12 kg of cherries were sold on Friday.

$$6 \times 3 \text{ kg} = 18 \text{ kg}$$

18 kg of cherries were sold on Saturday.

$$12 \text{ kg} + 18 \text{ kg} = 30 \text{ kg}$$

$$\begin{array}{r} {}^{1}1\,2 \\ +\,1\,8 \\ \hline 3\,0 \\ \hline \end{array}$$

<u>30</u> kg of cherries were sold on Friday and Saturday.

Example 2

Study the graph below carefully. The graph shows the type of fruit children like.

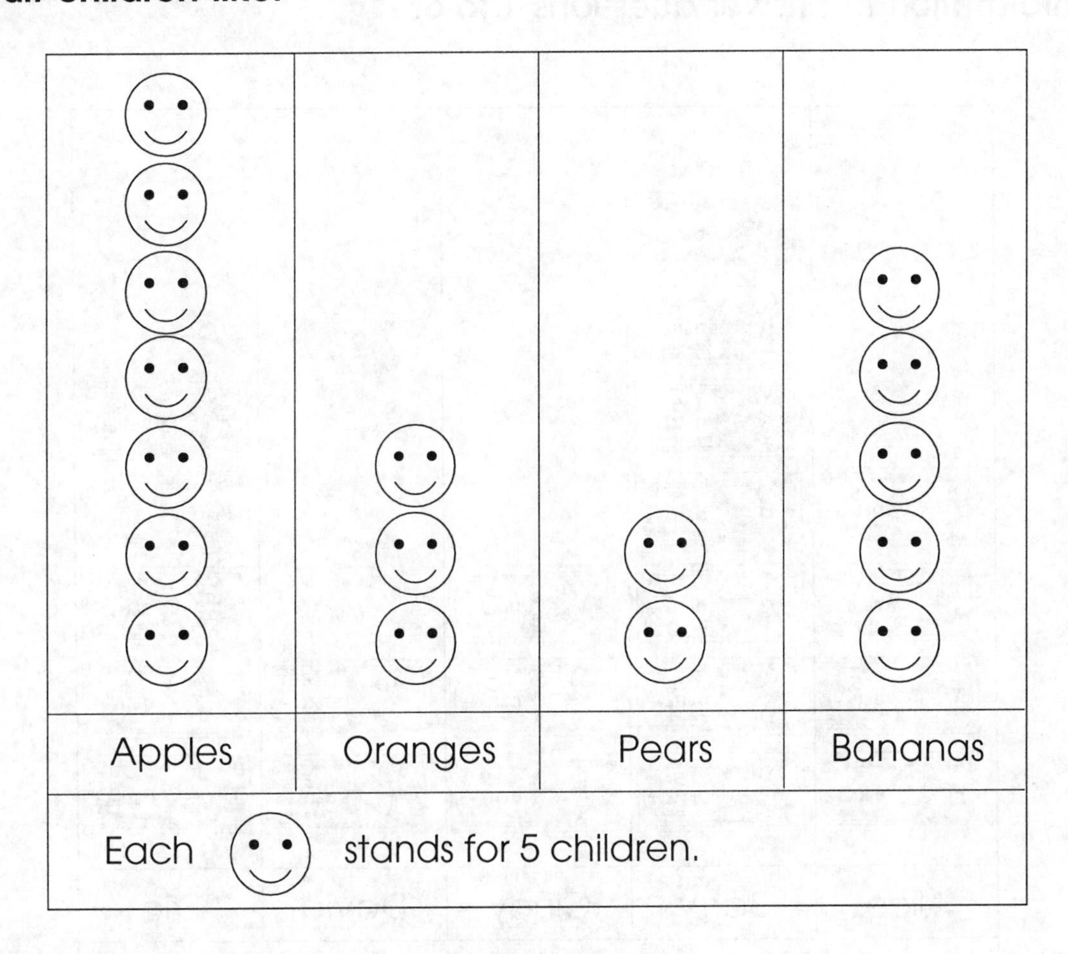

How many more children like apples than pears?

$$7 \times 5 = 35$$

35 children like apples.

$$2 \times 5 = 10$$

10 children like pears.

$$35 - 10 = 25$$

$$\begin{array}{r} 35 \\ -10 \\ \hline 25 \\ \hline \end{array}$$

25 more children like apples than pears.

PRACTICE

This picture graph shows the savings of 5 children. Use the information to answer questions 1 to 6.

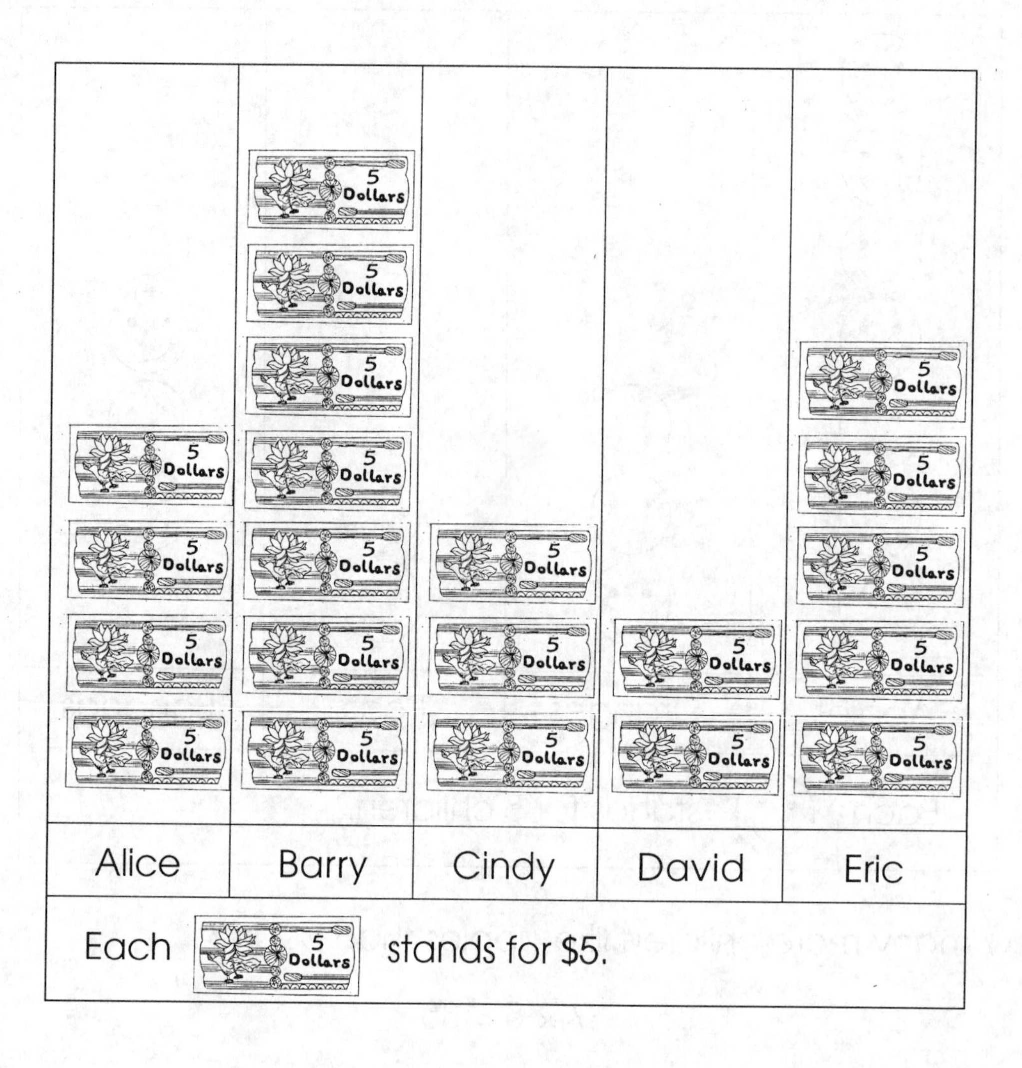

1. Who saves the most money?

2. How much money does Cindy save?

3. How much more money does Eric save than David?

4. Who saves twice as much as David?

5. Who saves $20 less than Barry?

6. How much money do the 5 children save altogether?

This picture graph shows the number of boys in each of the four Primary 2 classes. Study it carefully and answer questions 7 to 12.

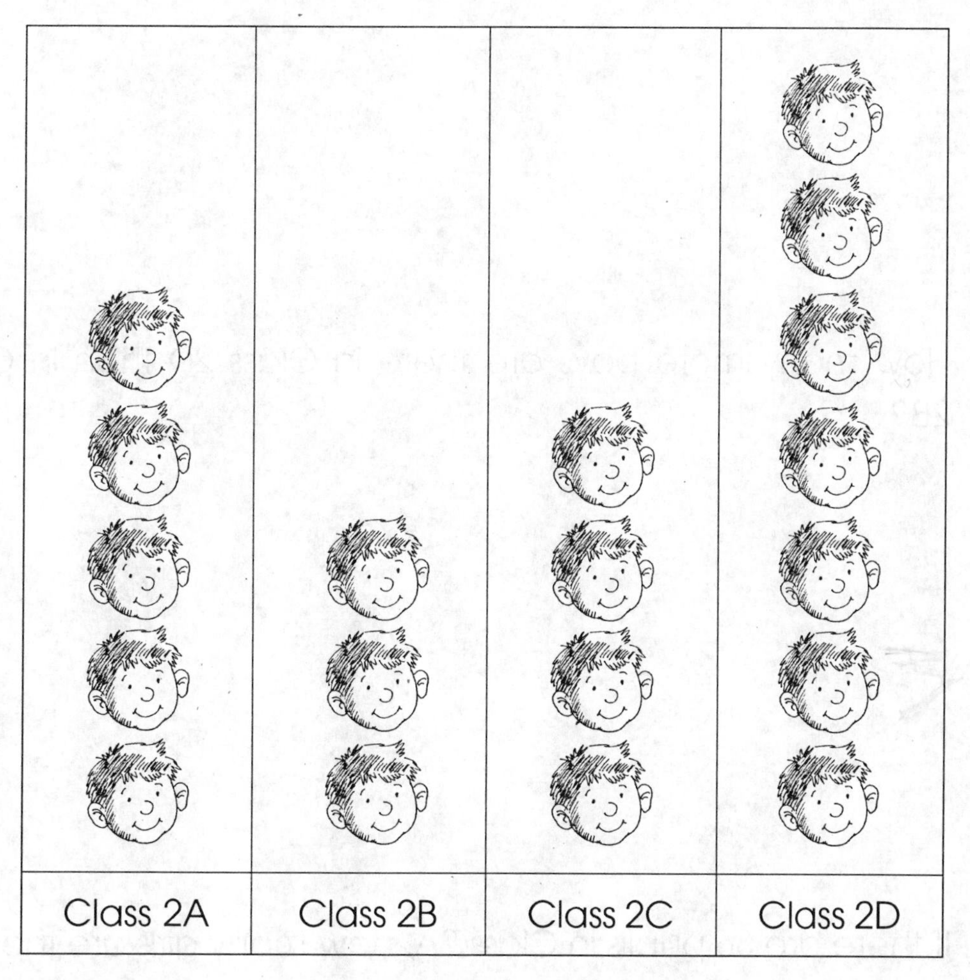

7. If there are 20 boys in Class 2A, what does each stand for?

8. How many boys are there in Class 2B?

9. How many more boys are there in Class 2D than in Class 2B?

10. If there are 36 pupils in Class 2A, how many girls are there in Class 2A?

11. There are 7 more girls than boys in Class 2C. How many pupils are there in Class 2C?

12. There are 145 pupils in the 4 classes altogether. How many girls are there in the 4 classes?

13. This table shows the number of eggs a cook used from Monday to Friday of a certain week. Use the information to complete the picture graph.

Day	Number Of Eggs Used
Monday	21
Tuesday	27
Wednesday	18
Thursday	15
Friday	30

Monday	
Tuesday	
Wednesday	
Thursday	
Friday	
Each ◯ stands for 3 eggs.	

Geometry

Example 1

The figure below is formed by straight lines and curves. How many straight lines and curves are there in the figure?

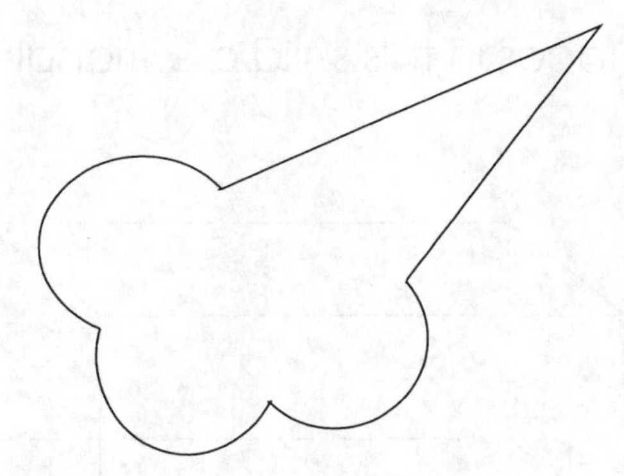

There are 2 straight lines and 3 curves in the figure.

Example 2

How many flat and curved faces are there in the object below?

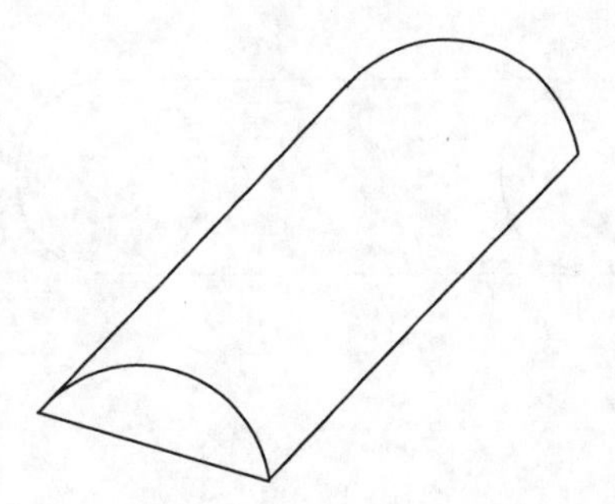

There are 3 flat faces and 1 curved face in the object above.

PRACTICE

1.

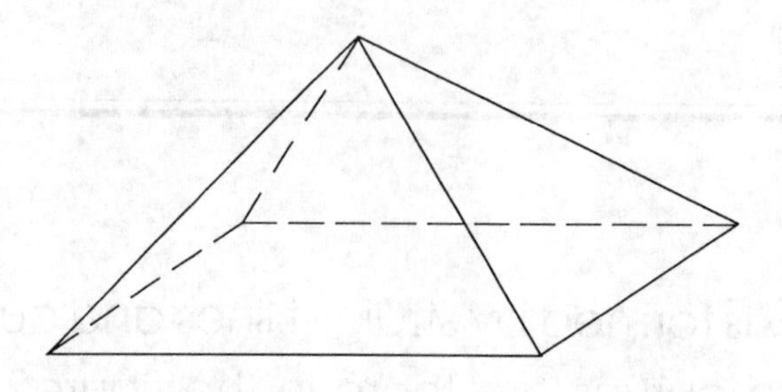

__________ faces in this solid are triangles.

2.

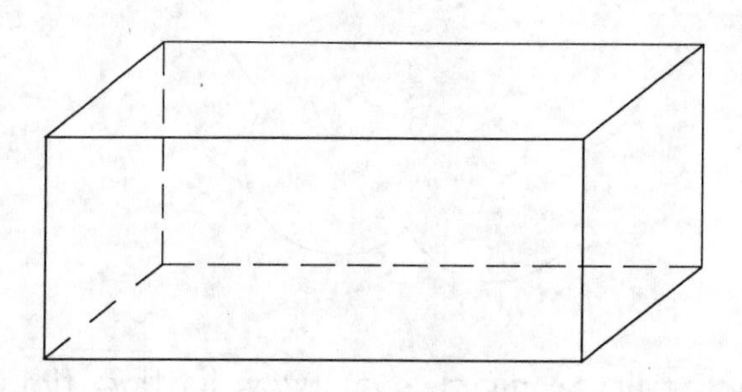

There are __________ faces in this solid.

3.

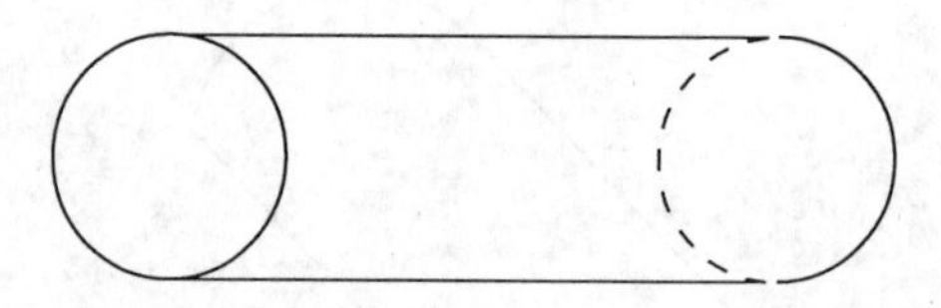

This solid has __________ flat face(s) and __________ curved face(s).

4.

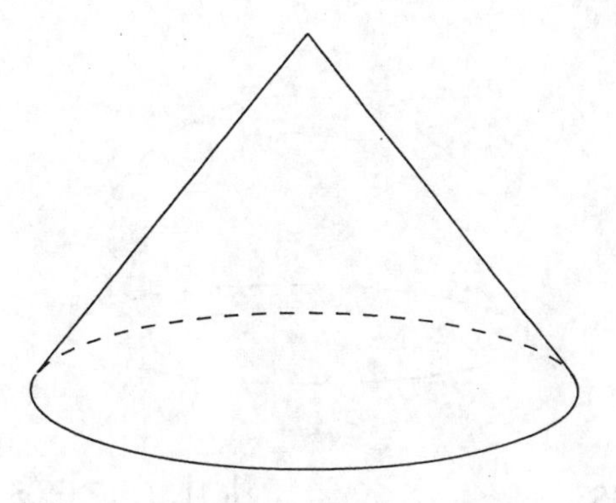

This figure has ____________ flat face(s) and ____________ curved face(s).

5.

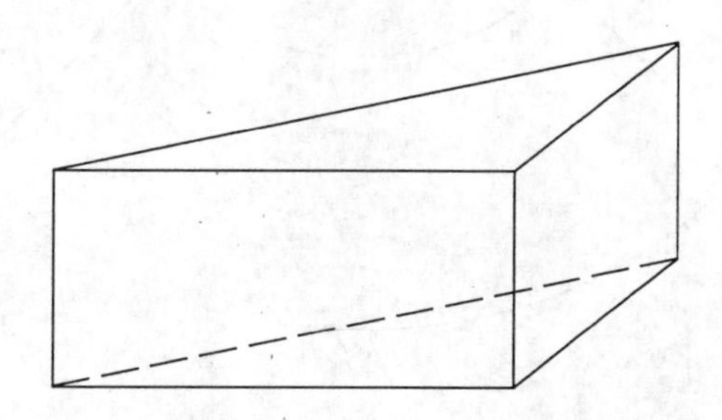

This figure has ____________ triangular face(s) and ____________ rectangular face(s).

6.

This figure has ____________ straight line(s) and ____________ curved line(s).

7.

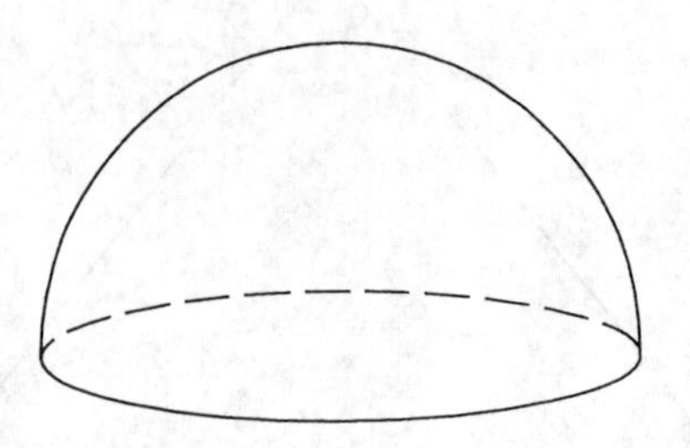

This figure has __________ flat face(s) and __________ curved face(s).

8.

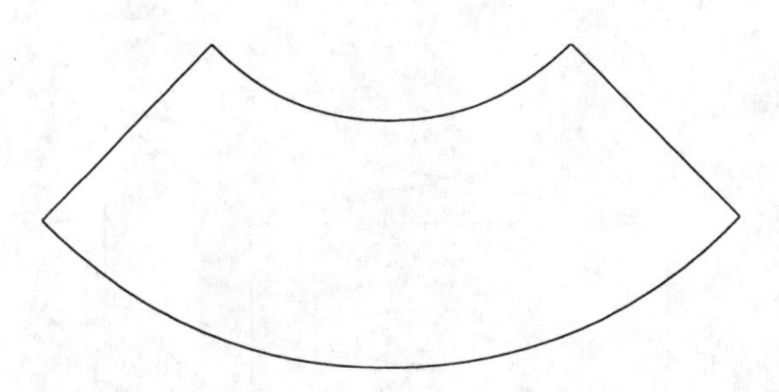

This figure has __________ straight line(s) and __________ curved line(s).

9.

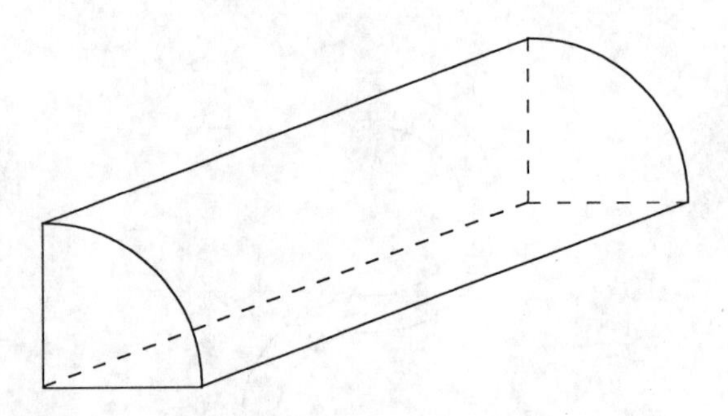

This figure has __________ flat face(s) and __________ curved face(s).

10.

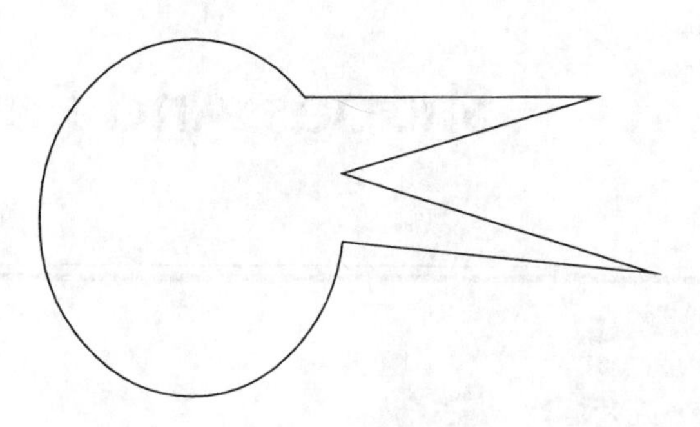

This figure has ____________ straight line(s) and ____________ curved line(s).

11.

This figure has ____________ flat face(s) and ____________ curved face(s).

12. Draw a figure that is made up of 4 straight lines and 4 curved lines in the box below.

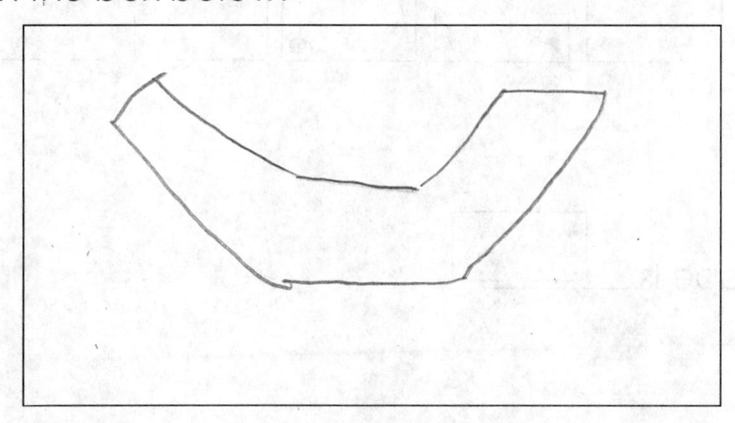

Shapes And Patterns

Example 1

Name the four shapes used to form the figure below.

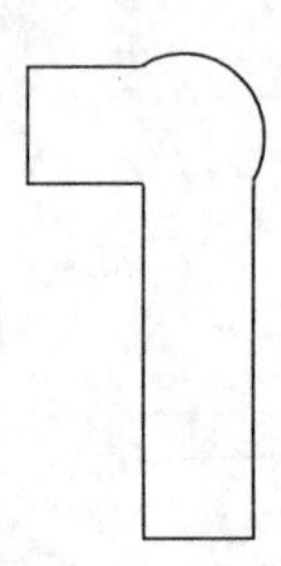

The four shapes are a square, a rectangle, a triangle and a semicircle.

Example 2

Study the pattern. What comes next?

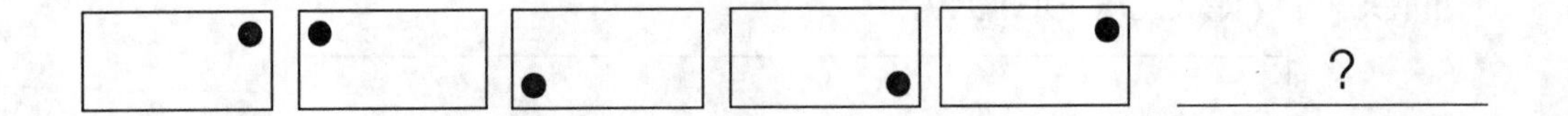

The next shape is ____________.

PRACTICE

Draw dotted lines to show the shapes that form each of the figures. Then name the shapes used to make each figure.

1.

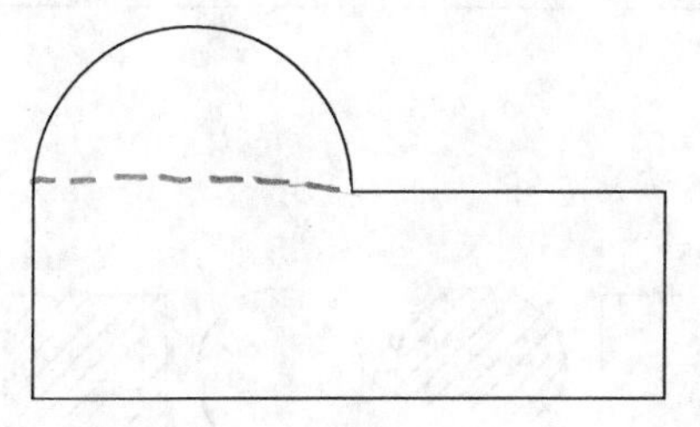

This figure contains a __________ and a __________.

2.

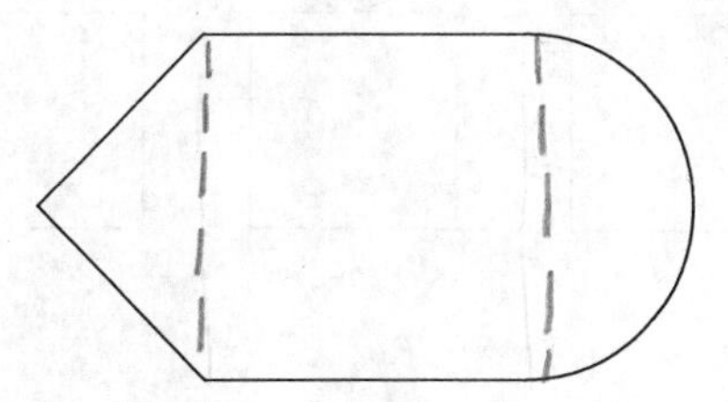

This figure contains a __________, a __________ and a __________.

3.

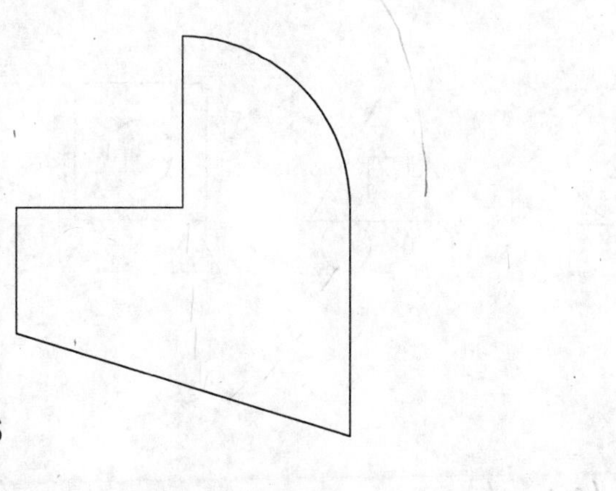

This figure contains a __________, a __________ and a __________.

For questions 4 to 12, complete the patterns.

4.

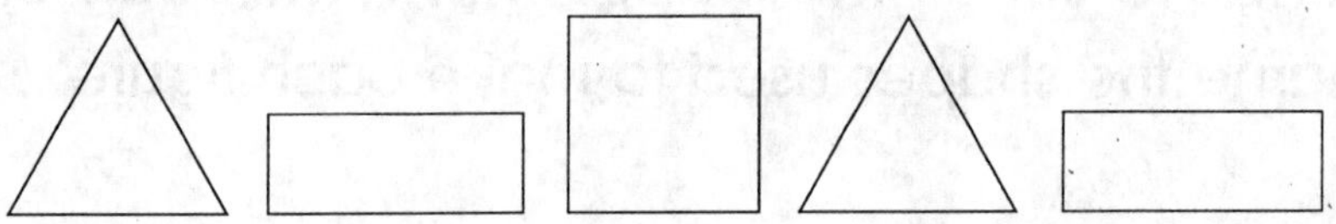

5.

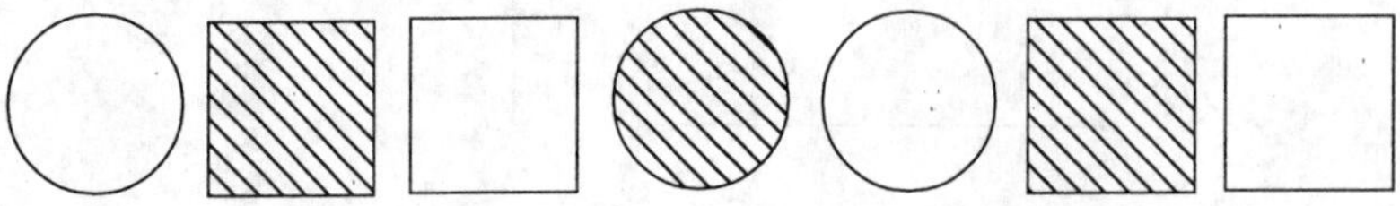

6.

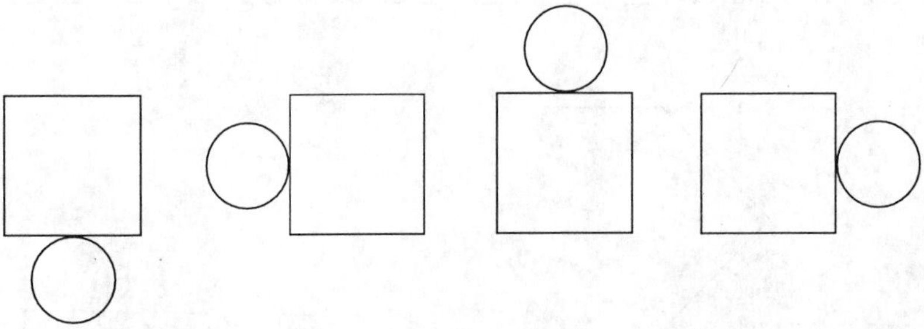

7.

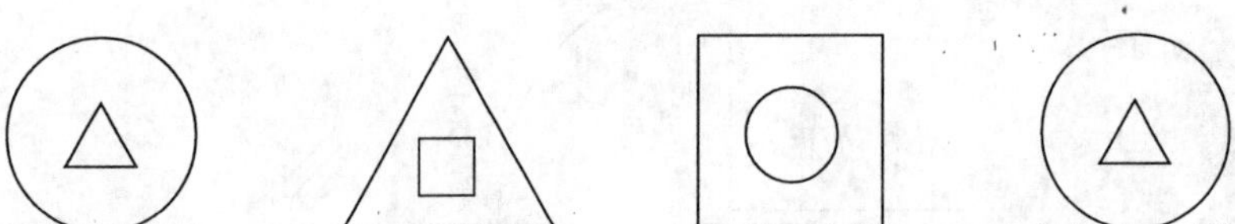

8.

9.

10.

11.

12.

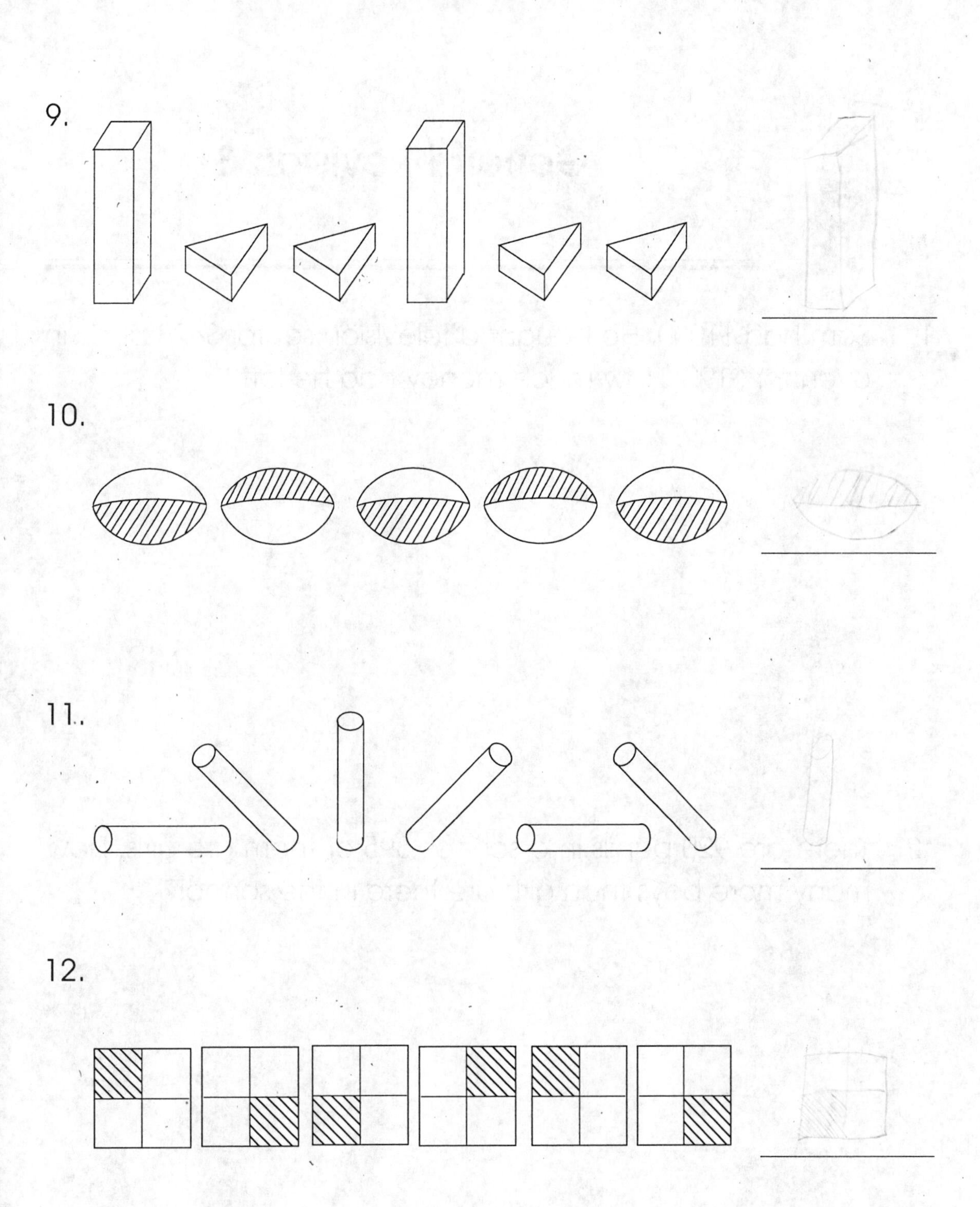

General Revision 3

1. Sam had $1000. He bought a television set for $428 and an oven for $192. How much money had he left?

*2. There are 920 pupils in a school. 395 of them are girls. How many more boys than girls are there in the school?

3. A piece of wire is 36 cm long. It is bent into a square. Find the length of each side of the square.

*4. Michelle had 314 red beads and 250 blue beads. She gave 97 red beads and 124 blue beads to her friends. How many beads had she left?

*5. Andy and Jeffrey spent an equal amount of money. Andy then had $162 more than Jeffrey. If Andy had $710 at first, how much money did Jeffrey have at first?

6. △ + △ = 10

○ × △ = 35

○ = ____________

*7. A baker made 102 tarts on Saturday. He made 99 more tarts on Sunday than on Saturday. How many tarts did he make on both days?

*8. Parcel A is heavier than Parcel B by 7 kg. Find the mass of Parcel A.

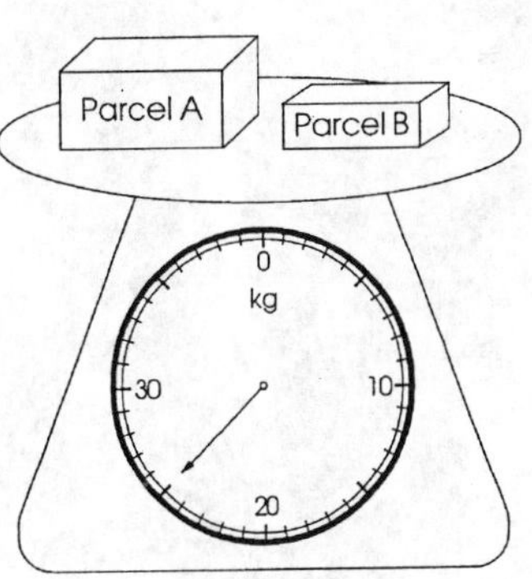

9. This clock face is 10 min fast. Find the actual time.

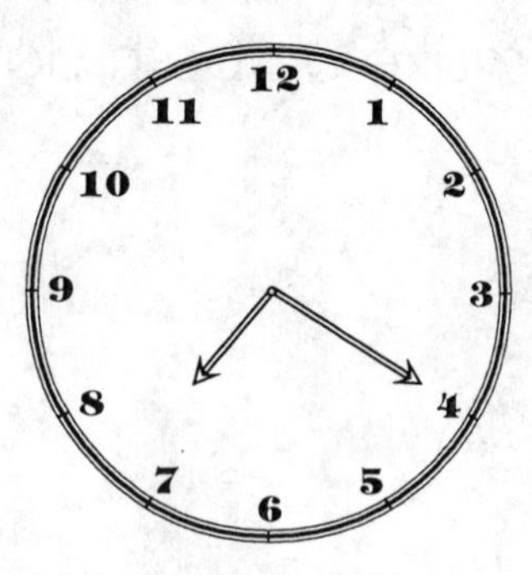

10. If △ △ △ △ stand for 20 pupils, then △ △ △ △ △ stand for ____________ pupils.

11. Kenny bought a pizza. He cut it into 6 equal pieces. He gave 2 pieces to Sam and 3 pieces to Suzie. What fraction of the pizza had Kenny left?

*12. Sharon had 13 five-dollar and two-dollar notes. 9 of them are two-dollar notes. Find the total value of the five-dollar and two-dollar notes.

General Revision 4

1. Mrs White bought a box of sweets. She gave 10 sweets to each of her 4 children and had 97 sweets left. How many sweets were there in the box at first?

*2. Mark has 9 stamps. Alice has 4 times as many stamps as Mark. How many stamps do both of them have altogether?

3. Peter has $129 more than Tom. Sandy has $87 less than Peter. If Tom has $357, how much money does Sandy have?

4. Paul had $9.75. He spent some money on food and had $7 left. How much money did he spend on food?

5.

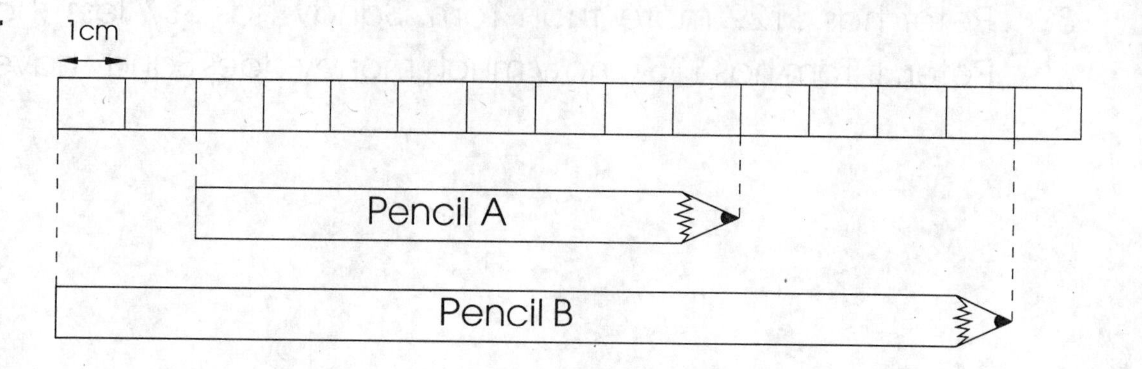

Find the total length of Pencil A and Pencil B.

*6. Elaine bought a hamburger. She gave the cashier a five-dollar note and received a change of 1 fifty-cent coin and 2 twenty-cent coins. How much did the hamburger cost?

7. What fraction of this square is shaded?

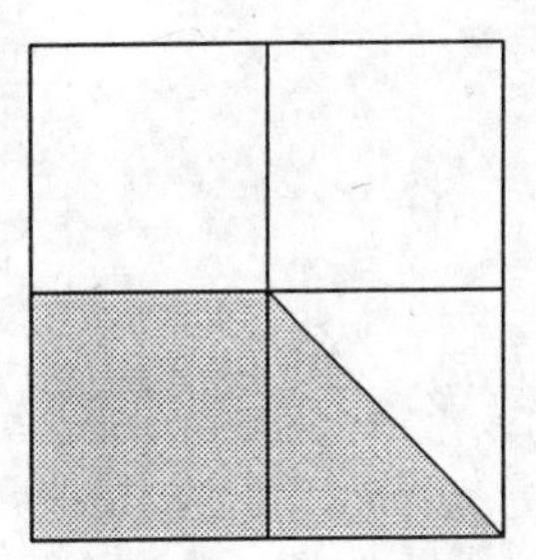

8. How many flat faces are there in this solid?

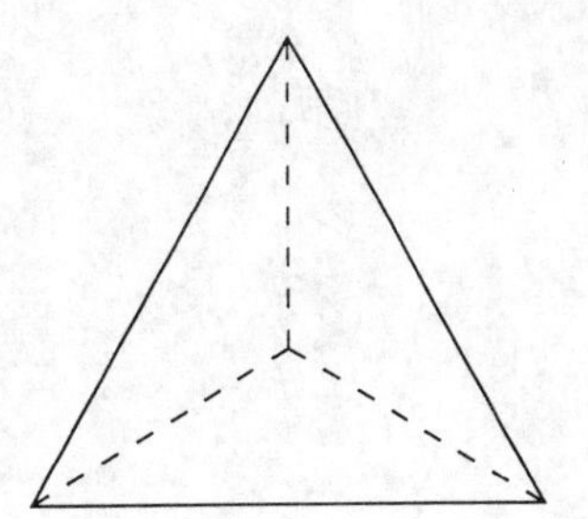

9. A tennis game began at 7.15 p.m. It lasted for 1 h 15 min. At what time did the tennis game end?

10. A handbag costs $59 more than a wallet. If the wallet costs $45, find the total cost of both items.

11. 5 jugs of water are needed to fill a pail. If each jug can hold 4 ℓ of water, how many litres of water can the pail hold?

*12. Sam has 36 balloons. Peter has 18 balloons. How many balloons must Sam give to Peter so that both of them will have an equal number of balloons?

Answers

Maths Problem-Solving Strategies Book 2

TOPIC 1

1. 397 + 504 = 901
   There are 901 pupils in the school.

2. $900 – $245 = $655
   The television set cost $655.

*3. 405 + 398 = 803
   Shirley had 803 blue and red beads.

   803 – 142 = 661
   She had 661 beads left.

4. 129 + 294 + 184 = 607
   Benny bought 607 paper clips.

5. 302 + 418 = 720
   The larger number is 720.

*6. 740 – 257 = 483
   The farmer has 483 chickens.

   483 – 257 = 226
   There are 226 more chickens than ducks.

7. 137 + 205 + 492 = 834
   He sold 834 fish altogether.

8. 900 – 82 = 818
   He used 818 straws to weave the basket.

9.

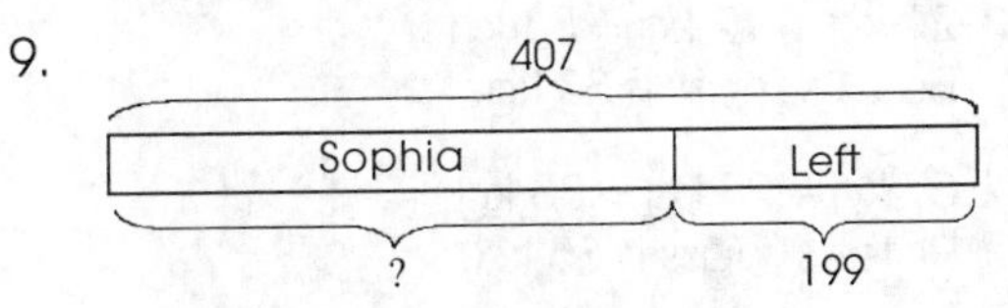

   407 – 199 = 208
   Marian gave 208 stamps to Sophia.

*10. $247 + $425 = $672
   The total savings of Paul and Adam is $672.

   $1000 – $672 = $328
   Samuel saved $328.

*11. ✿ + 310 = 455
   ✿ = 455 – 310
   = 145

   145 + ♣ = 424
   ♣ = 424 – 145
   = 279

   The value of ♣ is 279.

12. 920 – 359 = 561
   He sold 561 tarts on the second and third day altogether.

TOPIC 2

1. 94 cm + 16 cm = 110 cm
   James' height is 110 cm.

*2. 77 cm – 25 cm = 52 cm
   The red ribbon is 52 cm long.

   77 cm + 52 cm = 129 cm
   The total length of the two ribbons is 129 cm.

3. 358 m + 499 m = 857 m
   He travelled a total distance of 857 m.

*4. 102 cm + 13 cm = 115 cm
   Barry is 115 cm tall.

   115 cm – 29 cm = 86 cm
   Pete's height is 86 cm.

5. 425 m – 197 m = 228 m
   David must climb 228 m to reach the top of the hill.

*6. 640 cm – 294 cm = 346 cm
   Pole B is 346 cm long.

   346 cm – 294 cm = 52 cm
   Pole B is 52 cm longer than Pole A.

7. 75 cm + 109 cm = 184 cm
   The length of the first and second piece is 184 cm.

243 cm – 184 cm = 59 cm
The length of the third piece is 59 cm long.

8. 250 m + 305 m = 555 m
Cindy walked a distance of 555 m.

555 m – 427 m = 128 m
Cindy walked 128 m farther than Jason.

*9. 97 cm + 49 cm = 146 cm
146 cm of the wooden plank was painted red and blue.

200 cm – 146 cm = 54 cm
54 cm of the wooden plank was painted yellow.

*10. 250 cm – 64 cm = 186 cm
String B is 186 cm long.

250 cm + 186 cm = 436 cm
The total length of both strings is 436 cm.

11. Eraser = 4 cm
Stapler = 6 cm
4 cm + 6 cm = 10 cm
The total length of the eraser and the stapler is 10 cm.

12. Pencil = 10 cm
Stapler = 6 cm
10 cm – 6 cm = 4 cm
The pencil is 4 cm longer than the stapler.

TOPIC 3

1. 925 g – 185 g = 740 g
The mass of the oil is 740 g.

2. 127 kg – 75 kg = 52 kg
The mass of the tricycle is 52 kg.

3. 500 g + 200 g + 200 g = 900 g
The mass of the packet of flour and the packet of sugar is 900 g.

900 g – 725 g = 175 g
The mass of the packet of sugar is 175 g.

*4. 82 kg – 39 kg = 43 kg
Tom's mass is 43 kg.

43 kg – 39 kg = 4 kg
Tom is 4 kg heavier than Michelle.

5. 700 g – 520 g = 180 g
The mass of the mango is 180 g.

6. The mass of the brick is 270 g.

*7.

1 unit
8 kg
Rice
Flour
24 kg

24 kg – 8 kg = 16 kg
2 units have a total weight of 16 kg.

16 kg ÷ 2 kg = 8 kg
1 unit has the weight of 8 kg.

8 kg + 8 kg = 16 kg
The mass of the packet of rice is 16 kg.

*8.

2 ×
= 6 kg
= 12 kg ------------ (A)
= 14 kg ------ (B)

Comparing (A) and (B):

= 14 kg – 12 kg
= 2 kg

The mass of is 2 kg.

9. 320 g + 180 g = 500 g
She bought 500 g of strawberries.

500 g + 320 g = 820 g
The total mass of the grapes and strawberries that Mrs Lee bought is 820 g.

10. 50 kg – 29 kg = 21 kg
Kelly's mass is 21 kg.

21 kg + 12 kg = 33 kg
Barry's mass is 33 kg.

*11. 59 kg – 24 kg = 35 kg
Peter's mass is 35 kg.

35 kg – 24 kg = 11 kg
Peter is 11 kg heavier than Sally.

*12. 750 g – 510 g = 240 g
The mass of half a glass of water (excluding the glass) is 240 g.

510 g – 240 g = 270 g
The mass of the glass when it is empty is 270 g.

TOPIC 4

1. $18 \div 2 = 9$
   There are 9 boys in each team.

2. $21 \div 3 = 7$
   Each girl receives 7 cookies.

3. $18 \div 3 = 6$
   Maureen receives 6 stickers.

4. $3 \times 9 = 27$
   Mrs Wilson bought 27 apples altogether.

*5. $14 + 16 = 30$
   David had 30 marbles altogether.

   $30 \div 3 = 10$
   There were 10 marbles in each box.

*6. $2 \times 9 = 18$
   There were 18 chicken pies in 2 boxes.

   $18 - 3 = 15$
   15 chicken pies were left.

*7. $3 \times 8 = 24$
   The carpenter uses 24 screws for 3 stools.

   $35 - 24 = 11$
   He has 11 screws left.

8. $7 \times 2 = 14$
   He eats 14 eggs in one week.

9. $12 \div 3 = 4$
   Mervyn has 4 tricycles.

*10. $12 + 6 = 18$
   There are 18 children in the classroom.

   $18 \div 3 = 6$
   There are 6 groups.

*11. $3 + 7 = 10$
   There were 10 people at the birthday party.

   $10 \times 2 = 20$
   20 pieces of cake were eaten.

   $20 + 29 = 49$
   There were 49 pieces of cake at first.

12. $21 \div 3 = 7$
   There are 7 tables.

TOPIC 5

1. $7.30 – $0.30 = $7
   She spent $7 on food.

*2. $16 – $12 = $4
   The cost of the pen is $4.

   $16 + $4 = $20
   The cost of the pen and the storybook is $20.

   $40 – $20 = $20
   Charles had $20 left.

3. $8.25 + $0.90 = $9.15
   Alex saved $9.15.

4. 2 × $10 = $20
   Two ten-dollar notes make $20.

   $20 – $17.50 = $2.50
   He received $2.50 in change.

*5. $1 + $0.60 = $1.60
   The cost of the chicken burger is $1.60.

   $1.60 + $1 = $2.60
   The total cost of both items is $2.60.

*6. $9 – $6 = $3
   Dennis had $3 left.

   $5.90 – $0.50 = $5.40
   Paul had $5.40 left.

   $5.40 – $3 = $2.40
   Paul had left $2.40 more than Dennis.

*7. $10 – $9.50 = $0.50
   The can of soft drink cost $0.50.

   $7.70 – $0.50 = $7.20
   Xavier had $7.20 left.

8. 50¢ + 50¢ = $1.00
   Two fifty-cent coins make $1.00.

   20¢ + 20¢ + 20¢ = $0.60
   Three twenty-cent coins make $0.60.

   5¢ + 5¢ + 5¢ = $0.15
   Three five-cent coins make $0.15.

   $1.00 + $0.60 + $0.15 = $1.75
   She has $1.75.

9. $2.70 + $0.45 = $3.15
   The watermelon costs $3.15.

*10.

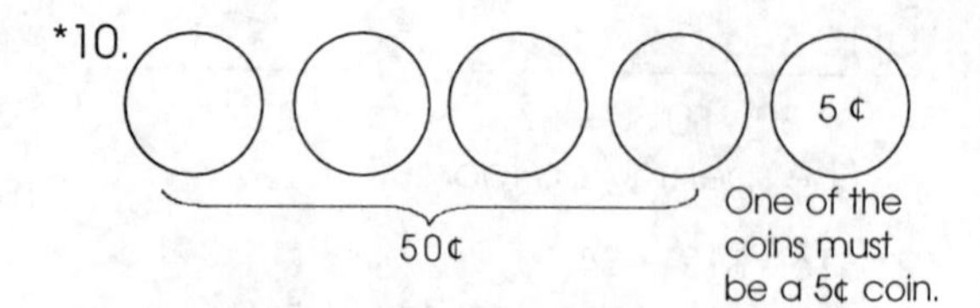

Use guess-and-check method:

First try: (10¢) (10¢) (10¢) (10¢) ✗

2nd try: (20¢) (20¢) (10¢) (10¢) ✗

3rd try: (20¢) (10¢) (10¢) (10¢) ✓

Monica has 3 ten-cent coins.

*11. 16 ÷ 2 = 8
There were 8 sets of durians.

8 × \$3 = \$24
She paid \$24 for the durians.

*12. \$27 ÷ 3 = \$9
Each person receives \$9.

2 × \$9 = \$18
Jacky and Tom receive \$18 altogether.

GENERAL REVISION 1

1. 495 + 379 = 874
There are 874 pupils altogether.

874 – 147 = 727
727 pupils do not wear spectacles.

2. \$379 + \$95 = \$474
He bought the camera and the pair of shoes for \$474.

\$750 – \$474 = \$276
Martin had \$276 left.

*3. 29 + 162 = 191
The number of broken eggs and left over eggs was 191.

974 – 191 = 783
He sold 783 eggs.

4. 142 – 55 = 87
Paul collected 87 seashells.

142 + 87 = 229
Both boys collected 229 seashells altogether.

5. 92 cm – 57 cm = 35 cm
Its breadth is 35 cm.

6. Pen = 11 cm
Scissors = 6 cm
11 + 6 = 17
The total length of the pen and the pair of scissors is 17 cm.

*7. 995 kg – 870 kg = 125 kg
The total mass of Mr and Mrs Lee is 125 kg.

125 kg – 72 kg = 53 kg
Mrs Lee's mass is 53 kg.

8. 21 kg ÷ 3 = 7 kg
The mass of each bag of rice is 7 kg.

2 × 7 kg = 14 kg
The mass of 2 bags of rice is 14 kg.

*9. 3 × 3 = 9
Daniel bought 9 handkerchiefs.

9 × \$2 = \$18
Daniel spent \$18 on the handkerchiefs.

10. 6 × 2 = 12
12 badminton players participated in the competition.

11. 70¢ + 30¢ = 100¢
= \$1
She spent \$1 on sweets and drink.

\$12 – \$1 = \$11
She had \$11 left.

12. \$7.45 – \$5 = \$2.45
He needs \$2.45 more.

GENERAL REVISION 2

1. 39 + 47 = 86
Mark gave away 86 marbles.

145 – 86 = 59
Mark had 59 marbles left.

*2. 452 – 195 = 257
There are 257 girls in the school.

452 + 257 = 709
There are 709 pupils in the school.

*3.

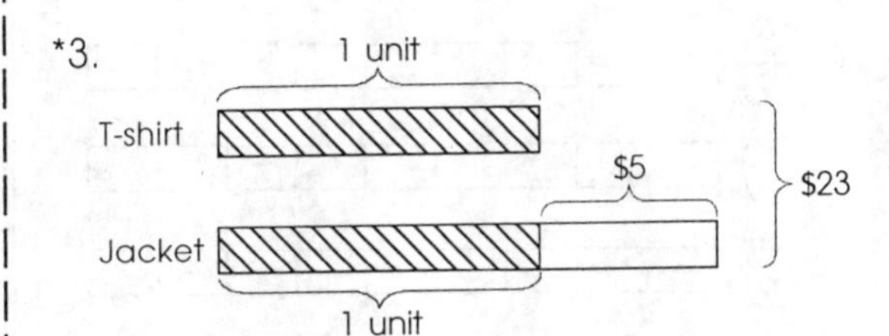

$23 – $5 = $18
Two units have a total cost of $18.

$18 ÷ 2 = $9
The T-shirt costs $9.

4. 102 + 295 + 340 = 737
He sold 737 durians in the 3 days.

5. Eraser = 3 cm
Pencil = 15 cm
15 cm ÷ 3 cm = 5
The pencil is 5 times longer than the eraser.

6. 13 cm + 24 cm = 37 cm
Ken is 37 cm taller than Mary.

7. 500 g + 200 g = 700 g
The mass of the 250 g weight and the packet of coffee powder is 700 g.

700 g – 250 g = 450 g
The mass of the packet of coffee powder is 450 g.

*8. 27 kg + 4 kg = 31 kg
William's mass is 31 kg.

27 kg + 31 kg = 58 kg
Jerald and William weigh 58 kg.

74 kg – 58 kg = 16 kg
Irene's mass is 16 kg.

9. 24 ÷ 3 = 8
Each child receives 8 sweets.

10. 18 ÷ 2 = 9
There were 9 guests at the party.

*11. $3.90 + $4 = $7.90
Julie had $7.90.

$7.90 – $0.35 = $7.55
She had $7.55 left.

12. $0.60 + $0.70 = $1.30
The total cost of the slice of watermelon and the stick of jackfruits is $1.30.

TOPIC 6

1. 4 × 7 = 28
Mrs Trent stayed in Japan for 28 days.

*2. 5 × 8 = 40
There were 40 pencils altogether.

40 – 12 = 28
He had 28 pencils left.

3. 9 × 5 = 45
45 people can be seated at the park at one time.

*4. 4 + 3 = 7
There were 7 children.

$35 ÷ 7 = $5
Each of them paid $5.

5. 45 cm ÷ 5 cm = 9
Anna had 9 pieces.

*6. 6 × $4 = $24
6 bottles of milk cost $24.

$59 – $24 = $35
He has $35 left.

*7. $100 – $72 = $28
The pens cost $28.

$28 ÷ $7 = 4
She bought 4 pens.

8. 9 × $10 = $90
They donated $90 to the orphanage altogether.

9. 40 ÷ 4 = 10
The cost of 1 wallet is $10.

3 × $10 = $30
The cost of 3 such wallets is $30.

*10. 9 × 5¢ = 45¢
9 five-cent coins make 45¢.

8 × 10¢ = 80¢
8 ten-cent coins make 80¢.

45¢ + 80¢ = 125¢
= $1.25
The total value of Kenny's coins is $1.25.

11. 4 × 9 = 36
She had 36 pieces of cake.

*12. $4 \times \$6 = \$24$
4 large durians cost $24.

$5 \times \$4 = \$20$
5 small durians cost $20.

$\$24 + \$20 = \$44$
The total value of the durians is $44.

$\$50 - \$44 = \$6$
She received $<u>6</u> in change.

TOPIC 7

1. $\underline{\frac{3}{8}}$ of the circle is shaded.
   <u>3</u> out of <u>8</u> equal parts are shaded.

2. $\underline{\frac{4}{5}}$ of the figure is shaded.
   <u>4</u> out of <u>5</u> equal parts are shaded.

3.

4.

5.

6.
   $\underline{\frac{1}{4}}$ of the bar is shaded.

7.
   $\underline{\frac{3}{5}}$ of the bar is shaded.

8.

9. $\frac{4}{5}$ (circled)
   $\frac{1}{5}$
   $\frac{3}{5}$

10. $\frac{1}{3}$
    $\frac{1}{2}$ (circled)
    $\frac{1}{5}$

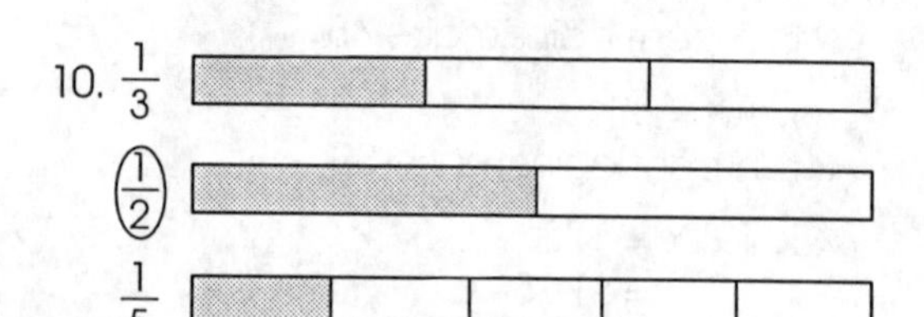

11. $\frac{2}{9}$
    $\frac{7}{9}$ (circled)
    $\frac{3}{9}$

12. $\frac{1}{6}$
    $\frac{1}{10}$ (circled)
    $\frac{1}{4}$

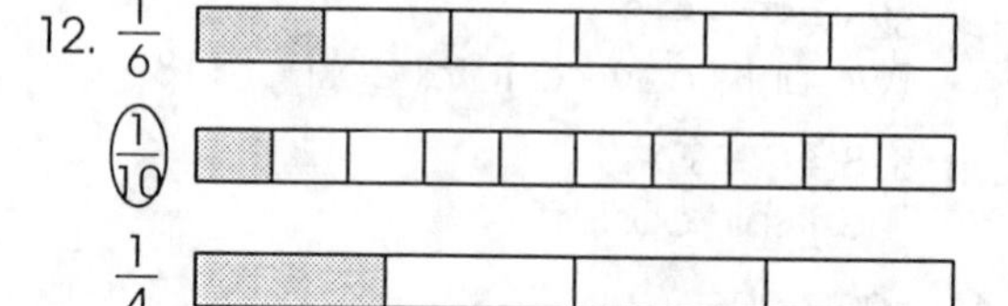

13. $\frac{3}{5}$
    $\frac{1}{5}$ (circled)
    $\frac{4}{5}$

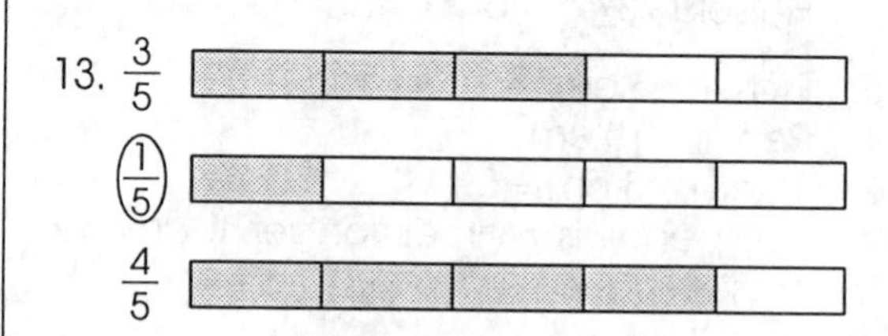

14. $\frac{5}{10}$
    $\frac{3}{10}$ (circled)
    $\frac{7}{10}$

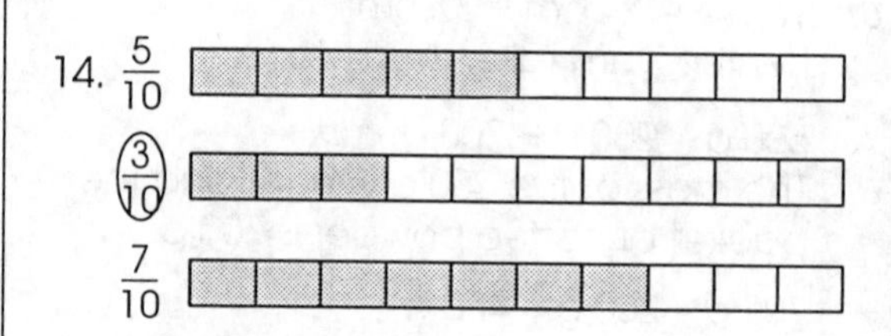

15. $\frac{1}{5}, \frac{2}{5}, \frac{3}{5}, \frac{4}{5}$

16. There are <u>4</u> quarters in one whole.

17. $\underline{\frac{1}{9}}$ is the smallest.

18. 3 pieces out of 8 equal pieces = $\frac{3}{8}$
    She had eaten $\underline{\frac{3}{8}}$ of the cake.

*19. Altogether, there are 9 parts.
     $9 - 4 = 5$
     5 parts are not shaded.
     Therefore, $\underline{\frac{5}{9}}$ of the circle is not shaded.

*20. $12 - 5 = 7$
     There are 7 girls.
     Therefore, $\underline{\frac{7}{12}}$ of the pupils are girls.

TOPIC 8

1. 8.25 + 1 h = 9.25
   The actual time is 9.25.

2. 2.00 + 30 min = 2.30
   The actual time is 2.30.

3. 5.50 – 10 min = 5.40
   The actual time is 5.40.

4. 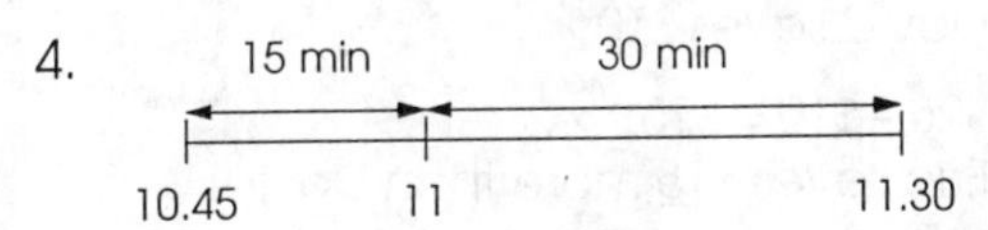

   15 min + 30 min = 45 min
   There are 45 minutes between 10.45 and 11.30.

5. 7.30 a.m. – 1 h = 6.30 a.m.
   He began cycling at 6.30 a.m.

6. 8.20 p.m. + 2 h = 10.20 p.m.
   The movie ended at 10.20 p.m.

*7. 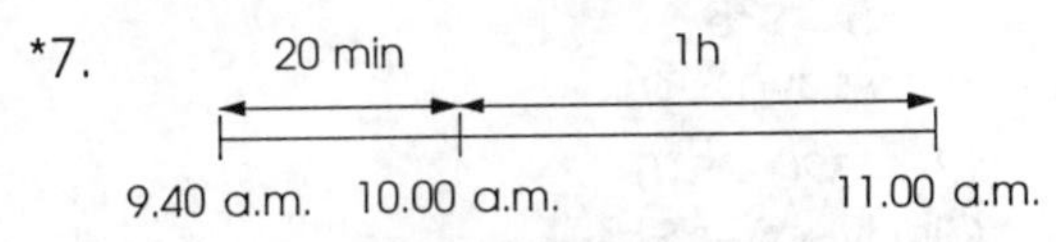

   The English test began at 9.40 a.m.

8. 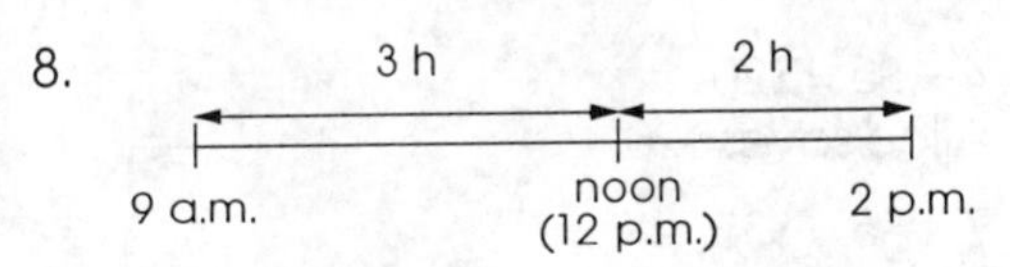

   3 h + 2 h = 5 h
   The coach travelled for 5 hours.

*9.
   40 min   10 min
   6.20 a.m.   7 a.m.   7.10 a.m.

   6.20 a.m. + 50 min = 7.10 a.m.
   He completed his jogging at 7.10 a.m.

10. 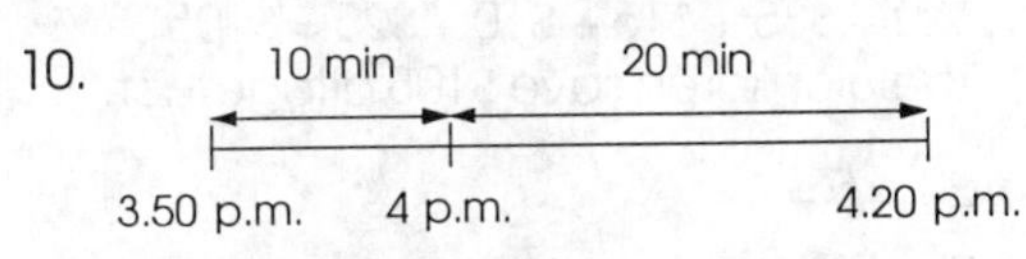

   3.50 p.m. + 30 min = 4.20 p.m.
   She woke up at 4.20 p.m.

11.
   20 min
   11.10 p.m.   11.30 p.m.

   The time shown on Derrick's watch is 11.10 p.m.

*12.
   30 min   1 h   15 min
   8.30 p.m.   9.00 p.m.   10.00 p.m.   10.15 p.m.

   1 h + 30 min + 15 min = 1 h 45 min
   He took 1 h 45 min to complete his homework.

TOPIC 9

1. 5 × 2 ℓ = 10 ℓ
   The jug can hold 10 ℓ of water.

2. 10 × 2 ℓ = 20 ℓ
   The tank can hold 20 ℓ of water.

   7 × 2 ℓ = 14 ℓ
   The pail can hold 14 ℓ of water.

   20 ℓ – 14 ℓ = 6 ℓ
   The tank can hold 6 ℓ more water than the pail.

3. Tank = 20 ℓ
   Jug = 10 ℓ
   20 ℓ ÷ 10 ℓ = 2
   The tank can hold 2 times as much water as the jug.

4. 10 × 2 ℓ = 20 ℓ
   The tank can hold 20 ℓ of water.

   7 × 2 ℓ = 14 ℓ
   The pail can hold 14 ℓ of water.

   6 × 2 ℓ = 12 ℓ
   The bottle can hold 12 ℓ of water.

   20 ℓ + 14 ℓ + 12 ℓ = 46 ℓ
   The total capacity of the tank, the pail and the bottle is 46 ℓ.

5. 9 × 4 ℓ = 36 ℓ
   David had 36 ℓ of paint.

   36 ℓ – 24 ℓ = 12 ℓ
   He had 12 ℓ of paint left.

*6. $65\ \ell - 32\ \ell = 33\ \ell$
Tank B contains 33 ℓ of water.

$65\ \ell + 33\ \ell = 98\ \ell$
The total amount of water in both tanks is 98 ℓ.

7. $12\ \ell + 9\ \ell = 21\ \ell$
Mary had 21 ℓ of mixed fruit juice.

$21\ \ell - 5\ \ell = 16\ \ell$
She had 16 ℓ of mixed fruit juice left.

*8. $5 \times 10\ \ell = 50\ \ell$
Mrs Andrews had 50 ℓ of oil in the large tins.

$9 \times 5\ \ell = 45\ \ell$
She had 45 ℓ of oil in the small tins.

$50\ \ell + 45\ \ell = 95\ \ell$
Mrs Andrews bought 95 ℓ of oil altogether.

*9. $40\ \ell - 5\ \ell = 35\ \ell$
She poured 35 ℓ of chocolate drink into 7 bottles.

$35\ \ell \div 7 = 5\ \ell$
There were 5 ℓ of chocolate drink in each bottle.

*10. $20\ \ell + 16\ \ell = 36\ \ell$
Mr Woods had 36 ℓ of petrol at first.

$36\ \ell \div 4 = 9\ \ell$
There were 9 ℓ of petrol in each tin.

*11.

1unit 4 ℓ
Pail
Basin
24 ℓ
1unit

$24\ \ell - 4\ \ell = 20\ \ell$
2 units have a total volume of 20 ℓ of water.

$20\ \ell \div 2 = 10\ \ell$
There are 10 ℓ of water in the basin.

12. $20\ \ell \div 5 = 4\ \ell$
Each pail holds 4 ℓ of water.

$2 \times 4\ \ell = 8\ \ell$
Two such pails can hold 8 ℓ of water.

TOPIC 10

1. Barry saves the most money.

2. $3 \times \$5 = \$15$
Cindy saves $15.

3. $5 \times \$5 = \$25$
Eric saves $25.

$2 \times \$5 = \$10$
David saves $10.

$\$25 - \$10 = \$15$
Eric saves $15 more than David.

4. $2 \times \$5 = \$10$
David saves $10.

$\$10 \times 2 = \$20$
Alice saves $20.

$\$20 \div \$10 = 2$
Therefore, Alice saves twice as much as David.

5. $7 \times \$5 = \$35$
Barry saves $35.

$\$35 - \$20 = \$15$
Cindy saves $15.
Therefore, Cindy saves $20 less than Barry.

6. $4 \times \$5 = \$20$
Alice saves $20.

$7 \times \$5 = \$35$
Barry saves $35.

$3 \times \$5 = \$15$
Cindy saves $15.

$2 \times \$5 = \$10$
David saves $10.

$5 \times \$5 = \$25$
Eric saves $25.

$\$20 + \$35 + \$15 + \$10 + \$25 = \$105$
The 5 children save $105 altogether.

7. $20 \div 5 = 4$
Each stands for 4 boys.

8. $3 \times 4 = 12$
There are 12 boys in Class 2B.

9. $7 \times 4 = 28$
   There are 28 boys in Class 2D.

   $3 \times 4 = 12$
   There are 12 boys in Class 2B.

   $28 - 12 = 16$
   There are 16 more boys in Class 2D than in Class 2B.

10. Number of boys in Class 2A = 20
    $36 - 20 = 16$
    There are 16 girls in Class 2A.

*11. $4 \times 4 = 16$
    There are 16 boys in Class 2C.

    $16 + 7 = 23$
    There are 23 girls in Class 2C.

    $16 + 23 = 39$
    There are 39 pupils in Class 2C.

12. $20 + 12 + 16 + 28 = 76$
    There are 76 boys in the 4 classes.

    $145 - 76 = 69$
    There are 69 girls in the 4 classes.

13.

Monday	○ ○ ○ ○ ○ ○ ○
Tuesday	○ ○ ○ ○ ○ ○ ○ ○ ○
Wednesday	○ ○ ○ ○ ○ ○
Thursday	○ ○ ○ ○ ○
Friday	○ ○ ○ ○ ○ ○ ○ ○ ○ ○
Each ○ stands for 3 eggs.	

TOPIC 11

1. 4 faces in this solid are triangles.
2. There are 6 faces in this solid.
3. This solid has 2 flat faces and 1 curved face.
4. This figure has 1 flat face and 1 curved face.
5. This figure has 2 triangular faces and 3 rectangular faces.
6. This figure has 2 straight lines and 2 curved lines.
7. This figure has 1 flat face and 1 curved face.
8. This figure has 2 straight lines and 2 curved lines.
9. This figure has 4 flat faces and 1 curved face.
10. This figure has 4 straight lines and 1 curved line.
11. This figure has 2 flat faces and 1 curved face.
12. (Suggested answer only.)

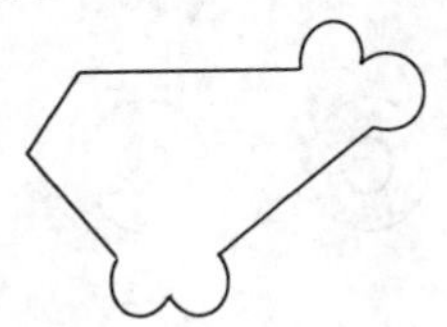

TOPIC 12

1.

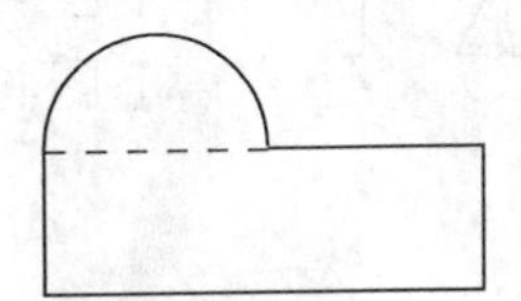

This figure contains a semicircle and a rectangle.

2.

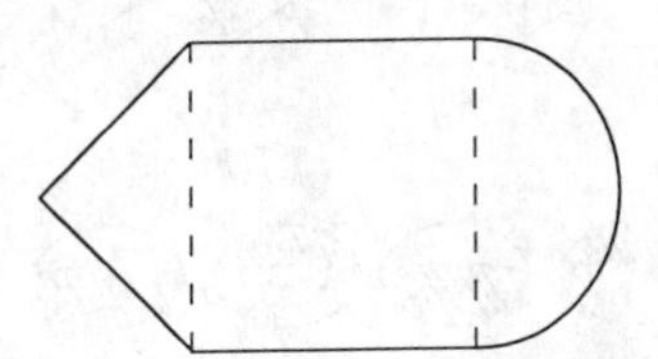

This figure contains a triangle, a square and a semicircle.

3.

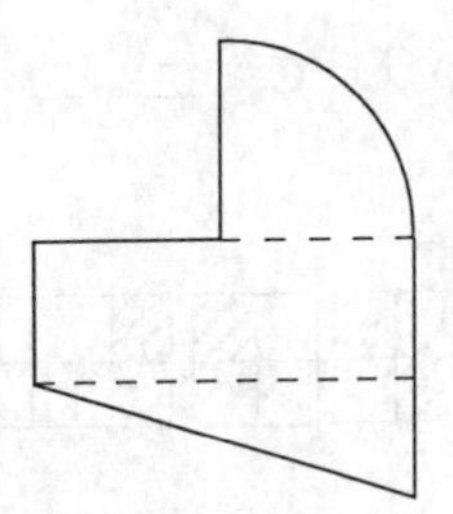

This figure contains a quarter circle, a rectangle and a triangle.

4.

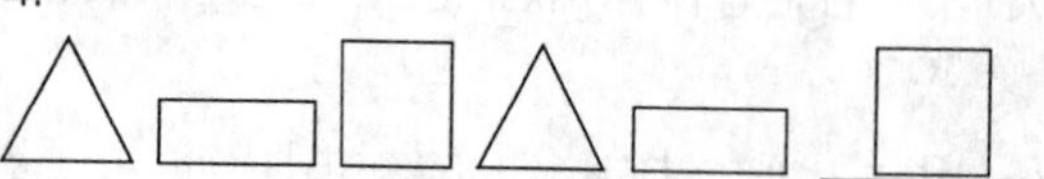

5.

6.

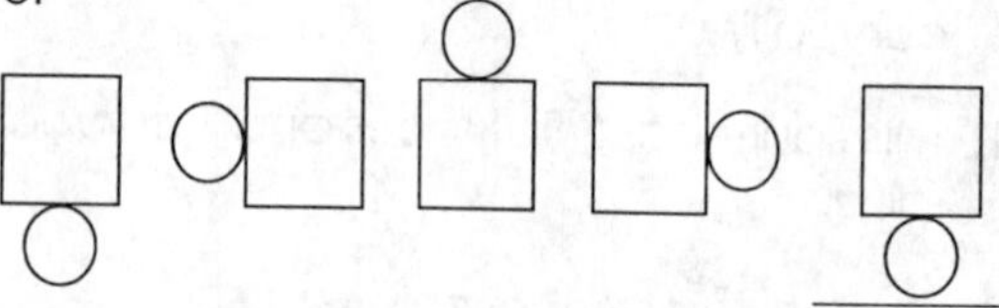

7.

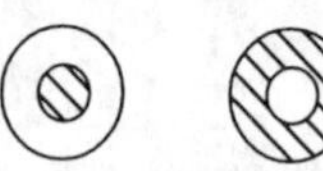 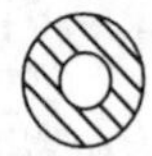 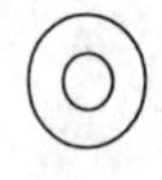 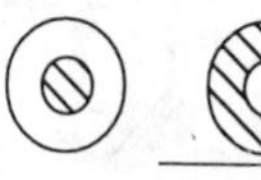

8.

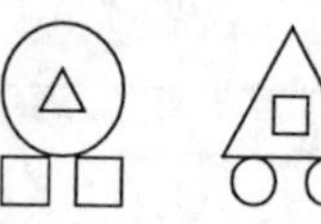 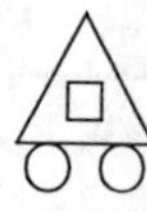 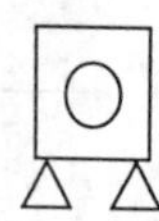 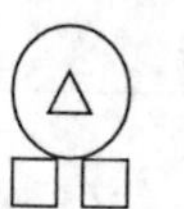 

9.

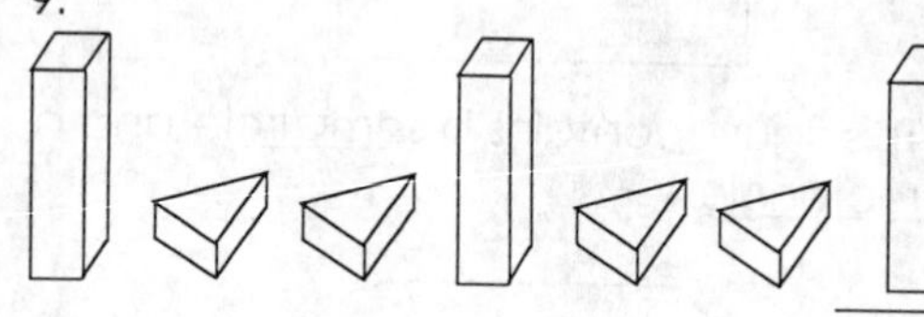

10.

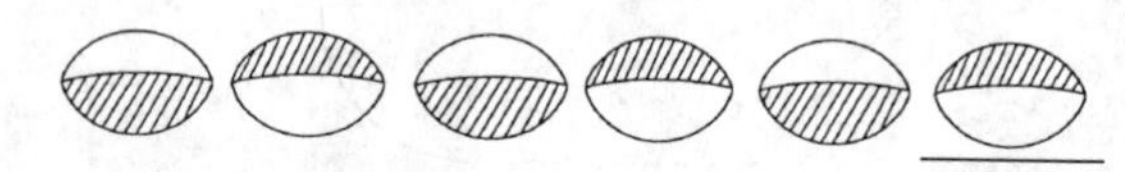

11.

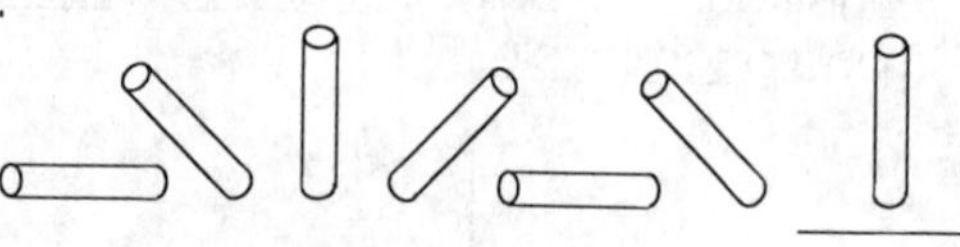

12.

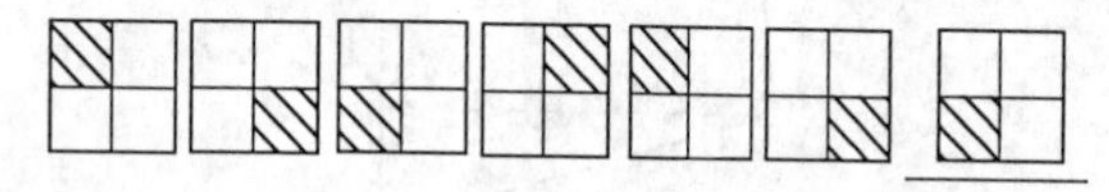

GENERAL REVISION 3

1. $428 + $192 = $620
   Sam paid $620 for the television set and oven.

   $1000 – $620 = $380
   He had $380 left.

*2. 920 – 395 = 525
   There are 525 boys.

   525 – 395 = 130
   There are 130 more boys than girls in the school.

3. 36 cm ÷ 4 = 9 cm
   The length of each side of the square is 9 cm.

*4. 314 + 250 = 564
   Michelle had 564 red and blue beads.

   97 + 124 = 221
   She gave 221 beads to her friends.

   564 – 221 = 343
   She had 343 beads left.

*5. $710 – $162 = $548
   Jeffrey had $548 at first.

6. 10 ÷ 2 = 5
   Each triangle (△) stands for 5.

   35 ÷ 5 = 7
   The circle (○) stands for 7.

*7. 102 + 99 = 201
   The baker made 201 tarts on Sunday.

   102 + 201 = 303
   He made 303 tarts on both days.

*8.

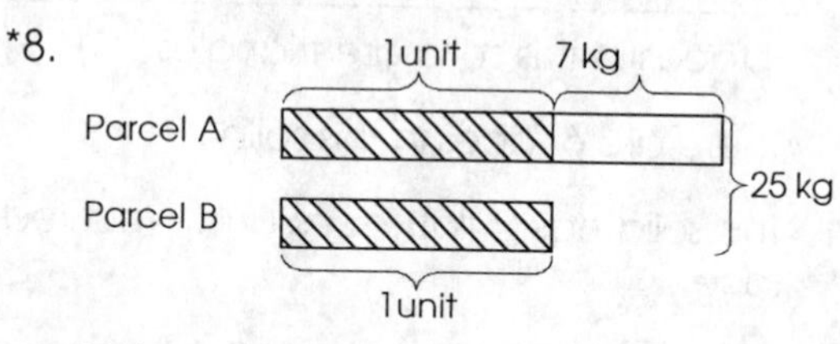

25 kg – 7 kg = 18 kg
2 units have a total weight of 18 kg.

18 kg ÷ 2 = 9 kg
1 unit has a weight of 9 kg.

9 kg + 7 kg = 16 kg
The mass of Parcel A is 16 kg.

9. 7.20 – 10 min = 7.10
   The actual time is 7.10.

10. △△△△ = 20 pupils
    △ = 20 ÷ 4
    = 5 pupils
    △△△△△ = 5 × 5
    = 25 pupils

11. 6 – 2 – 3 = 1
    Kenny had 1 piece left.
    Therefore, Kenny had $\frac{1}{6}$ of the pizza left.

*12. 9 × $2 = $18
    Sharon had $18.
    13 – 9 = 4
    She had 4 five-dollar notes.
    4 × $5 = $20
    She also had $20.
    $18 + $20 = $38
    The total value of the five-dollar and two-dollar notes is $38.

GENERAL REVISION 4

1. 4 × 10 = 40
   4 children received 40 sweets.
   40 + 97 = 137
   There were 137 sweets in the box at first.

*2. 9 × 4 = 36
   Alice has 36 stamps.
   9 + 36 = 45
   Both of them have 45 stamps altogether.

3. $129 + $357 = $486
   Peter has $486.
   $486 – $87 = $399
   Sandy has $399.

4. $9.75 – $7 = $2.75
   He spent $2.75 on food.

5. Pencil A = 8 cm
   Pencil B = 14 cm
   8 cm + 14 cm = 22 cm
   The total length of Pencil A and Pencil B is 22 cm.

*6. $0.20 + $0.20 = $0.40
   2 twenty-cent coins make $0.40.
   $0.50 + $0.40 = $0.90
   She received $0.90 in change.
   $5.00 – $0.90 = $4.10
   The hamburger cost $4.10.

7. $\frac{3}{8}$ of the square is shaded.

8. There are 4 flat faces in this solid.

9. 1 h, 15 min
   7.15 p.m. — 8.15 p.m. — 8.30 p.m.
   The tennis game ended at 8.30 p.m.

10. $45 + $59 = $104
    The handbag costs $104.
    $45 + $104 = $149
    The total cost of both items is $149.

11. 5 × 4 = 20
    The pail can hold 20 ℓ of water.

*12. 36 – 18 = 18
    Sam has 18 more balloons than Peter.
    18 ÷ 2 = 9
    Sam has to give 9 balloons to Peter so that both of them will have an equal number of balloons.